# TWENTY SNOBS AND MAO
*Travelling de luxe in Communist China*

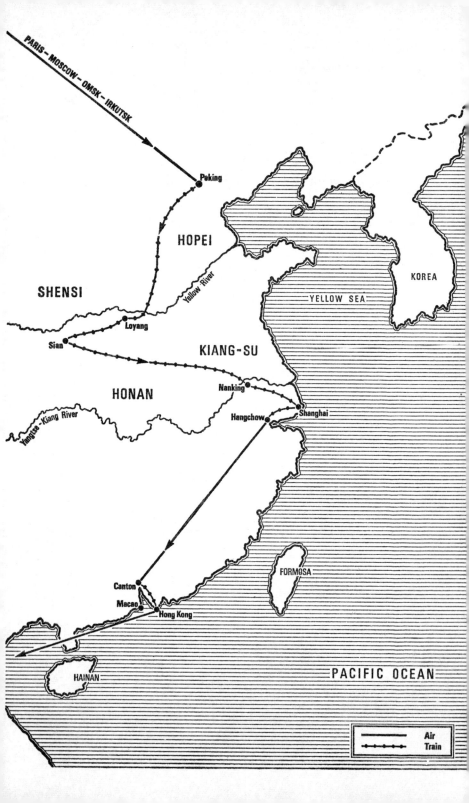

# Twenty Snobs and Mao

## Travelling de luxe in Communist China

### COLETTE MODIANO

Translated from the French by
JACQUELINE BALDICK

READERS UNION
MICHAEL JOSEPH
*London* 1970

*This R.U. edition was produced in* 1970 *for sale to its members only by the proprietors, Readers Union Limited, at Aldine House,* 10-13 *Bedford Street, London W.C.*2 *and at Letchworth Garden City, Herts. Full details of membership may be obtained from our London address.*

*Originally published by Michael Joseph Ltd.*
*Printed for Readers Union by Hollen Street Press Limited at Slough.*

*To my Clémentine*

# ILLUSTRATIONS

# LIST OF CHARACTERS

THE FRENCH 'MANDARINS'
  The Author
  Monsieur Pariet—the artistic adviser
  Charlotte Florent—the part-time French Mandarin in Peking

THE CHINESE
  Yuan—the chief interpreter. A Party member
  Shin—also a student
  Shu—probably 'the eyes of Peking' ... and the ears

THE ITALIANS
  Marquis Torti and Signora Coli—'Two is company ...'
  Signora Leandri—the widow of a diplomat
  Signora Negri—the wife of a Milanese industrialist and her
  beautiful daughter Isabella

THE MUSKETEERS
  Georges Wolf—the art gallery owner
  Alexandre Dupont—the gay Swiss
  Georges Noiret—the miniature emperor

THE 'NICE ONES'
  Countess de Castillat (Laure)
  Madame Quesnel (Colette)
  Doctor and Madame Blum
  Monsieur and Madame Adjouf
  Monsieur and Madame Chapeau
  Countess de Lissaye
  Señor and Señora Neralinda

THE OTHERS!
  Madame Mandois (Adrienne)
  General de Boilèle
  and Madame Trollan

# 1

Twenty faces suddenly turned towards the windows. A rumour had just run the length of the plane: thirty thousand feet below our Tupolev, a few hills had appeared in the distant haze, then a vast plain, and on the horizon, touched with pink by the rising sun, an agglomeration of buildings. In a mewing English accent the air hostess confirmed that 'over there is Peking'. My heart missed a beat. Peking! I had waited so long for this moment: two years of negotiations, one year of preparation, four days of chaotic travel. And now Peking was there, and with Peking that China of a thousand mysteries across which, for a whole month, I was going to trail the first members of the most expensive tour in the history of world travel, a Red tour for millionaires. There were twenty of them who had left their hunting-lodges in Sologne, their all-night revels at Régine's, their dinner-parties, Rolls Royces and fittings at Chanel's. Twenty members of the European upper crust who under my timid guidance were going to mix with Mao's human ants. A prospect which promised a few surprises.

I too had an old Chanel suit in my suitcase and my car wasn't a Volkswagen either. Nobody could really call me an intellectual and my left-wing principles had been known to desert me. Nor was I a graduate of the School of Oriental Languages. There was nothing, therefore, to draw me towards China—nothing but a mysterious fascination fed on childhood reading, a strong sense of curiosity, and an eagerness to find out, to find out all I could about that country. But oddly enough, during the next four weeks, I was to live on the frontiers of two worlds, the world of my twenty snobs and the world of the Chinese people, for the latter would regard me as the 'proletarian' of the group, the working-girl, the industrious shepherd of an exacting capitalist flock, a flock such as the Chinese had never met before.

Now the Tupolev was coming down to make a noisy, bumpy landing. A reception committee of Chinese buttoned up to the eyebrows in fawn or black gabardine suits were waiting impassively in the rain, clutching bunches of gladioli. A group of Yugoslavs were the first to emerge from the plane. The Chinese bowed, smiled, made speeches, listened to the replies, got rid of their gladioli and led away their visibly daunted guests.

We got out next, before the Negro students who filled the rest of the plane. Was there no reception committee for us? Yes, there was! In front of the gigantic bust of Mao in the lounge, a speaking likeness down to the wart on the chin, a smiling young man dressed in the usual high-necked gabardine uniform made a gracious speech of welcome in French. His name was Shin, and he was to be our chief interpreter throughout our tour. He was tall for a Chinese, and slim, with eyes that smiled behind his metal-rimmed glasses. He had long, delicate hands, and looked like an intellectual. He took me over to a man of about thirty, dressed all in black, with a long hard face. This man's name was Yuan. A big nose, thick lips, and dazzling teeth bared in a perpetual smile. His little hand held mine for a long time. Then, inspecting me with an absent-minded expression, he launched into a long monologue which Shin translated simultaneously into excellent French. Standing in front of my flock, who had collapsed on to the arms of easy chairs or on to their hand luggage, I listened unflinchingly.

'The Chinese People's Republic,' Yuan declared in conclusion, 'is happy to welcome its French friends and wishes them an interesting journey.'

I shifted from one foot to the other, slightly intimidated by the pompous side of this welcome. I followed on by expressing our joy at finding ourselves at long last 'on the soil of this great country'. To which Yuan replied:

'We have the same desire as you: to make this tour a success. We want to show you everything, the things of the past as well as our modern achievements.'

I seized my chance, for I knew all too well how hard you had to fight in China to see museums and pagodas, whereas the Chinese insisted on giving their visitors a surfeit of factories and dams. In my warmest tone of voice I said:

'Thank you, Monsieur Yuan, for greeting us with such a splendid promise, for we have come a long way to visit your country. We have an equal interest in its astonishing past, its admirable present and its glorious future.'

Whew! With these words I hoped that the reception ceremony would come to an end and we should at last be able to go to our hotel. I was wrong. Yuan remained solidly planted on his little legs, put on a broader smile than ever, and launched out yet again:

'We have a great deal to learn from our French friends, and will regard as a mark of friendship any criticism you are good enough to make about us.'

Glancing at the glum faces of my fellow travellers, I declared with verbal precautions worthy of Marco Polo that we were tired out and longing for a rest.

The square in front of the airport was covered with grass, flowers and trees. It was a gay, pretty sight, but it was raining and hot. We climbed into a very comfortable Czechoslovak coach, with tables provided with ashtrays and seats with white lace antimacassars on the headrests. A little Mongolian woman with irregular but attractive features came up to me. Dressed in a pair of trousers which looked like a jacket and a jacket which looked like a pair of trousers, she informed me in impeccable French that she was our second interpreter and that her name was Shu. During the whole journey she kept her narrow eyes fixed on my face and her hands implacably thrust in her pockets.

The coach crossed the western part of Peking along an avenue lined with trees planted, so Shin told me, 'since the Liberation'. That was almost certainly true: they were quite small, but graceful and leafy. Huge blocks of brick and concrete buildings separated by lawns and clumps of trees stood next to older houses, little whitewashed single-storey buildings with grey tiled roofs turned up at the edges, in accordance with an ancient Chinese tradition, to drive away evil spirits. Shin informed me disdainfully that all this would soon disappear to be replaced by wide avenues lined with huge apartment buildings of the kind we had just seen. 'Five years from now, all the old districts will have disappeared...' Not a single private car to be seen. The coach forced its way through a mass of bicycles, cycle-rickshaws and carts drawn by a horse, a donkey, an ox, a man ... or a woman. Not a single shout, not even a glance in the direction of our heavy vehicle and its capitalist cargo.

At the sight of a cycle-rickshaw Marquis Torti yelled:

'There's your Communism for you! I thought it meant everyone was equal, but here you've got people getting other people to pull them.'

A shiver went down my spine. But Shin retorted calmly that with the development of motor transport the cycle-rickshaw would gradually disappear.

The avenue was now lined with trees in blossom. A fine drizzle was falling. The air was dappled like the light in old prints We drove into the huge T'ien An Men Square on which the gigantic processions of the 1st of May and the 1st of October took place under the fatherly eye of the great god Mao. The square was flanked by two enormous buildings in the Stalinist style with tall square-cut columns: 'The People's Assembly and the Museum of the Revolution,' Shin announced proudly. The coach drove through some more districts of the capital. Here the houses seemed to have been stuck together by pure chance, without any perceptible pattern. They were survivals of a past in which the emperors reigning in Peking had cared about nothing but the Imperial City, so that, in the absence of an enlightened middle class capable of taking concerted action, every family had tried to satisfy its needs as best it could, in a state of total anarchy.

The fatigue of the journey made us extremely sensitive to the drabness of the city and its inhabitants as they hurried impassively along the wet streets. The men and women in the streets were all dressed in the same navy-blue cotton jackets and trousers, gabardine clothes being reserved for teachers, doctors, engineers and interpreters. But both cotton and gabardine, I later discovered, were rationed and were sold only in exchange for coupons. A worker was entitled to two cotton garments a year.

While I was looking around wide-eyed, trying to see everything, I was counting the stubs of the luggage tickets Shin had given to me at the airport. My heart missed a beat, for there was one suitcase unaccounted for! I had only fifty-five tickets instead of fifty-six. Trying to keep calm despite a presentiment of catastrophe, I counted again the stubs of the tickets I had been given in Moscow. There were fifty-six all right. This was terrible. What an appalling atmosphere it was going to create among my pilgrims! Which of them was I going to have to inform of the loss of his or her suitcase? In this austere country where they would have so little to amuse them, the incident was sure to assume traumatic proportions. They would hold me responsible for what had happened and I would lose all semblance of authority. Which of them would take the matter most to heart? I feared the worst, for by now I knew them fairly well. We were just beginning our fourth day together. And what days the previous three had been!

# 2

I had made their acquaintance at the traditional cocktail party
the organizers of the tour had given them a few weeks before
our departure. The atmosphere had been very high society.
Masses of questions such as 'What's the food like in China?' ...
'Is it cold out there?' ... 'Are there lots of things to buy?' A
painted sexagenarian brunette had even asked me whether she
should take her mink coat with her. Suddenly panic-stricken at
the idea of trailing these ferocious socialites across the land of
the dungaree, I had taken refuge among a few friendly faces:
a newspaper editor's widow, the proprietor of one of the leading
modern art galleries in Paris, and a mischievous-looking little
Swiss.

At Le Bourget, two weeks later, I planted myself a good hour
in advance in front of the desk of the Soviet company Aeroflot
which was to take us as far as Moscow. I was greeted with an
adamant *Niet* from the ground steward, who refused to accept
my forty pounds' excess luggage. I was taking clothes with me
that would stand up to all kinds of conditions, but I had also
packed a few rather more elegant things. I also had a small portable library of books on Chinese art and two shoe-boxes full of
medicines. The arrival of a uniformed, gold-braided, magnifi-
cently Slav superior put an end to the incident. With my luggage
registered I went and took up my position facing the main
entrance, feeling a slight sinking feeling in the pit of my stomach as I waited for my pilgrims.

The first to arrive were the Chapeaus, a somewhat provincial-
looking couple in their fifties. The husband, a northern industrialist with close-cropped grey hair and kindly blue eyes
lurking behind gold-rimmed glasses, was dressed in a grey check
suit with a rather over-long jacket. The wife, a woman with
short grey hair and a somewhat shabby camel-hair coat, hissed at

me in a shrill, affected voice: 'Good morning, Mademoiselle, are you our guide?' The 'Mademoiselle' cut me to the quick. I may not look my forty years, but I hate being treated as if I had been left on the shelf.

Next to show up was the dark, painted shrew I had met at the cocktail party, the one who wanted to take her mink coat with her. This was Adrienne Mandois. With her crimson ski-pants and matching boots, her black wig and her bright red lips, she looked like a vamp of the silent screen. Which was exactly what she was. She bore down upon us, simpering and smirking. In her wake came two porter-slaves laboriously dragging several trolleys loaded with suitcases.

'I like to change trousers every day,' she giggled.

'And boots too?' I asked laughingly.

'Of course. I've got some in velvet for the evening.'

'She must have varicose veins,' whispered Alexandre Dupont, the little Swiss with the comical Geneva accent who was to be my factotum throughout our tour.

Adrienne Mandois went on chattering away imperturbably. 'Laure!' she exclaimed in a burst of simpering affection, wringing the hand of the Countess de Castillat, a frail creature in her sixties who walked with the aid of a stick, whose head was crowned with a large red chignon, and whose delicately wrinkled face was lit up by a keen, blue-eyed, mocking gaze. The Countess de Lissaye, elegant and fair-haired, made a dashing entrance, haloed with small parcels.

All of a sudden there was a rush of people like the scramble for the last train on the Métro. They arrived all together in a jumble of luggage which I registered all together. Georges Wolf, the proprietor of a gallery of modern art, his black hair tousled like that of a wicked angel, laid five expensive suitcases at my feet in a homage I could well have done without. The Aeroflot ground steward seemed totally subjugated and resigned.

Shaking hands in the midst of a pyramid of suitcases, I started getting everyone mixed up, and to get rid of them I advised them to lay in a stock of whisky and cigarettes for the journey. Then there was a last-minute tussle with Aeroflot when they refused to take on board Pariet, our artistic adviser, claiming that he was not booked on the flight. This was the last straw. There were screams and shouts in two languages. Finally Aeroflot gave way once more and peace was restored.

I was the last to board the Tupolev, which took off with a terrifying, shuddering roar. After take-off I went around fussing over every member of my flock. On the way I was caught by Marquis Torti, a lanky, charming Italian of about sixty with a thin face furrowed by two vertical lines, a booming voice and inexhaustible eloquence. He gazed ecstatically at his companion, the very beautiful Signora Coli, an elegant woman getting on for fifty with sculptured features, high cheekbones and huge dark eyes. Marquis Torti had clearly appointed himself the protector of the Italian minority within our group, for he began lecturing poor Signora Leandri, a diplomat's widow who was sipping her vodka with contented hiccoughs. In the same row and within earshot of Marquis Torti was the wife of a Milanese industrialist, Signora Negri, an attractive middle-aged woman with a finely chiselled face, framed in grey hair which made her look like an eighteenth-century marquise. In the next seat her daughter Isabella was dreaming like a Botticelli. I sat down for a few moments at the front of the plane next to General de Boilèle. He shot an aquamarine glance at me which, lurking behind a scrub of grey eyebrows made him look like an old pirate. He bent his elegant stature towards his friend, Madame Trollan, whose haughty fifties had somewhat erased the glowing fairness praised twenty years ago by Parisian society. Barely acknowledging my polite inquiries, she disdainfully turned her magnificent head away and went on picking at her caviare.

As I continued on my rounds I felt the usual pang inseparable from the beginning of any tour: the feeling of being in a lions' den.

After a brief, confused stop at Moscow, we all crowded into another Tupolev, this time a single-class aircraft, which was to take us to Peking. My pilgrims were scattered among Negro students from Ghana and Rhodesia, and Cubans who were going to study at Peking University. My neighbour, a red-headed giant, looked like an American footballer. He was a Frenchman, never stopped laughing, had lived in the United States which he loved, and travelled every year to China which he adored. He told me dozens of fascinating stories about China. On the other side of the aisle, four Yugoslavs drank the last of my bottle of vodka. One of them spoke French very well and seemed very friendly. The other three lay right across him to ogle the legs of the pretty Italian girl, Isabella Negri. Ours was the lighthearted corner of the plane. In front of us the Negroes dozed in silence. So did the 'élite' of my party.

At two o'clock in the morning we touched down at Omsk, in Western Siberia. A fat hostess wedged herself into the aisle and barked that the plane would not be taking off again straight away. I had a sudden presentiment and advised my flock to take their hand luggage with them. Some of them objected. I insisted. They were to thank me later for my firmness.

A boneshaking bus deposited us in front of a sort of two-storey barracks block. Inside, going up a narrow concrete staircase, we found a long paved corridor lined with square, green-painted rooms, tiny cells nine feet wide furnished with two iron bedsteads, a washbasin, a chair and an electric light-bulb hanging from the ceiling. My pilgrims didn't wait to indulge in any useless courtesies. Each one rushed headlong into a room. The one which fell to me offered me the pleasant company of Signora Leandri, the Italian diplomat's widow. The poor woman was tormented by the idea that she might not have time to put on her corset again in the event of a sudden departure. I gave her my word of honour—shouting at the top of my voice, because she was as deaf as a post—that the plane wouldn't take off before she had time to pull her corset on.

The central heating was very capricious—the bedrooms were either scorching hot or icy cold—but there was a general atmosphere of gaiety. Nobody really felt like going to bed. The French Ambassador in Peking, who was travelling the same way, had joined us and was joking with my neighbour on the plane, who for his part had obviously taken the fancy of the painted vamp. I suddenly noticed a tall Russian, with crystal eyes and a tough jaw-line, who turned out to be the local Intourist agent. He informed me in monosyllables that we would not be leaving before five in the morning because of fog over Irkutsk, our next stop. Feeling rather pessimistic, for I had rarely seen a fog lift at five in the morning, I tucked my flock up for the night. In the meantime the Russians had filled the corridors with camp beds on which most of the coloured students were already asleep. The others watched me go by with a slightly hostile indifference. In front of the door of my room a pretty Cuban girl was stretched out on a mattress, reading Maupassant's *Bel Ami*. We chatted together for a few minutes. She was a gay, intelligent girl. I left her, feeling a little embarrassed at going to sleep in a real bed, wished my room-mate a good night, and promised to wake her up at least half an hour before departure, still on account of the corset.

We were woken up at eight in the morning by shouts from the Intourist representative, who pushed us, without a word of explanation, into the same boneshaking bus as the day before. Our first stop was the airport restaurant where trim waitresses in floral aprons served us a copious Siberian breakfast: bortsch, brown ale, kippers, sardines with onions, chicken and mashed potatoes, and creamy yoghourt. After the usual protestations—'I never eat anything in the morning'—everybody proceeded to do justice to the meal. The big dining-room with its tables covered with white cloths was full to bursting: peasant women in felt boots, wearing full cotton skirts in several thicknesses, sat holding their children wrapped up in huge woollen shawls. They had flat faces with high cheekbones and narrow slanting eyes. The men wore shiny grey overcoats and soft caps, while some of them, better off than the rest, had fur hats. Most of them were laden with huge baskets overflowing with vegetables, eggs, chickens, even live ducks. One tubby little man was actually carrying a piglet in his arms which was uttering shrill squeals. All these people were waiting with patient resignation for their plane. Some of them would be flying as far as Rostov, and even Moscow, to sell the produce of their private plot of land. Here, in the vast roadless expanses of Siberia, the plane plays the part of the bus in any other part of the world.

Boris, the Intourist ogre, announced in a rumbling growl: 'Fog at Irrrkutsk. Take-off postponed', and shepherded everybody back to the barracks we had hoped we should never see again. All around me, I could feel morale dropping to zero. I put on a brave smile, but I too was appalled by this fresh delay. China had never seemed so far away. All of a sudden the task of looking after these twenty *de luxe* tourists, with their pernickety ways and exacting requirements, struck me as an impossible burden. The Ambassador did his best to cheer me up: he smilingly told me that on his last trip he had been stuck at Irkutsk for four days. This finished me off.

The countryside all around was completely flat. In the golden morning air we could see the factory chimneys of Omsk smoking in the distance. A few small planes landed on a nearby airfield, and a suspicious guard appeared who ordered us with an imperious gesture to look the other way. At lunch-time we travelled out to the restaurant and back again, with Boris announcing in the same growling voice that he 'regrrretted' take-off was still delayed. I began to find the joke 'wear-r-ring' thin, and my companions were getting more irritable with every hour that passed. I begged Boris to organize a coach tour of Omsk to keep my impatient flock amused. This request brought forth an explosion of Slav fury: 'Omsk is closed to forrreigners!'

The noble game of bridge solved eight of my problems for a while, but our vamp kept complaining:

'I'm going to have to spend the rest of my life here, that's certain. We shall never be able to get away!'

'We ought to have gone through India,' moaned the Countess de Castillat. 'At least the weather's fine there.'

I reminded her that there had been a war between China and India not very long ago and that relations between the two countries were anything but cordial.

The atmosphere became painfully tense. But suddenly an idea occurred to me—to drown the boredom and relieve the tension in vodka. The ogre Boris uttered a fresh groan when I put my idea to him. Luckily one of my charges, a French doctor's wife from Casablanca who spoke perfect Russian, backed me up in my efforts to obtain the precious liquid. Dear, sweet Madame Blum! With her lovely smiling face and her long auburn hair tied in a chignon, she was the very picture of serenity. Boris surrendered to her charm and in return for forty dollars dug out four bottles of vodka. The evening promised to be more cheerful than I had expected. The corners of Signora Negri's mouth promptly turned up in a smile, and Signora Leandri was soon as red-faced as a country priest after a good meal. Everybody ended up by returning to his little green cell, slightly tipsy and in fairly good spirits.

My pretty Cuban girl was still in the corridor as well as the other students. None of them had been able to wash. I took advantage of my room-mate's intoxication to let the Cuban girl use our washbasin.

At eight o'clock we were once again woken up by Boris's dulcet tones. When the bus stopped again outside the restaurant my heart sank, and on our return to the barracks a minor revolt broke out among my flock.

'We're obviously going to stay here till we rot,' repeated Countess de Lissaye. 'What dreadful organization!'

'Why don't we take the Trans-Siberian?' asked Laure de Castillat. 'You must fix that up for us.'

'The Trans-Siberian takes a week,' I said impatiently. 'You have to have reservations, and above all visas which they can't give us here.'

'We ought to go back to Moscow,' suggested Colette Quesnel, 'and wait there for the fog to clear at Irkutsk.'

'We haven't got a visa for Moscow,' I snapped, 'and if we come back here and the fog comes down again at Irkutsk, we'll be back at Square One.'

Signora Negri suddenly gave a display of geographical expertise. 'Why don't we go through Pakistan?' she asked.

In the corridor I found myself surrounded by a screaming mob, under the startled gaze of the Ambassador. General de Boilèle called out to me through his open door and beckoned me into his room. Madame Trollan was sitting on the bed, scowling and beautiful. Boilèle stamped his foot and screamed at me:

'I order you to get the group together and tell them that if we haven't left Omsk by tonight we are going back to Paris.'

I suddenly lost my temper. I reminded everybody that I was the one who took decisions here, adding:

'Now that I've made that clear, if any one of you wishes to leave the group, you are welcome to do so, but you take all the consequences.'

A profound silence greeted these manly words. Boris summoned us to lunch. To help me, the Ambassador, who could see where the shoe was pinching, took charge of Madame Mandois. And very successfully too, to judge by the fluttering of her eyelashes.

A charming buxom blonde took over from Boris, who said goodbye to us with a stiff bow. I found her all the more charming in that she came and whispered in my ear that we should be leaving after lunch. When I gave the signal for departure—at the very last moment, for fear of yet another disappointment—the General patted me on the back and said:

'What did I tell you? I knew that everything would work out all right!'

The bus was taken by storm. Neralinda, a Peruvian banker

who had joined us at Moscow and who looked like a fat little chicken, launched into a lively conversation with the lovely Cuban communist, asking her countless questions about the subjects she was going to study in Peking. I caught sight of dark gleams from the wig Adrienne Mandois was shaking bewitchingly under the eyes of the Ambassador, who shot me a conspiratorial glance. The atmosphere was one of positive euphoria. It seemed the ideal moment to tell my flock that we would have to spend the night at Irkutsk, since that part of Siberia was not equipped for night flights. A storm of cheers greeted this piece of news which only two days earlier would have been regarded as a catastrophe.

'It will be amusing to see Irkutsk!'

This was splendid! I boarded the Tupolev feather-light with relief. Tired out, I fell asleep on my neighbour's enormous shoulder, which like the rest of him was encroaching on my seat.

Four hours later we were slithering in the muddy snow of the dimly lit airport of Irkutsk. Like the railway station of many a French village, this airport is situated at the end of a broad, gloomy avenue lined with trees and three-storey houses. After slipping about in the snow for two hundred yards, we entered the hall of the only house with lights on, to be greeted by a buxom creature bursting out of a black uniform with silver buttons. She bawled out the names of the passengers, allocating one room to every six names. How on earth were my *de luxe* passengers going to take this, I wondered, when some of them had paid out a handsome sum to have a room to themselves? Fearing the worst, I exaggerated the number of my charges, and obtained half-a-dozen rooms which I shared out as best I could.

I put together the three men I privately called the Musketeers: Georges Wolf, the art-gallery owner, Alexandre Dupont, the little Swiss, and Noiret, a little man who had given me a bit of a headache on a tour of Egypt on which he had taken a sulky blonde he had tried to impress with his dictatorial attitudes. As he brushed forward over his forehead what little hair he had left, he reminded me, with his pointed nose and his tiny round eyes, of a miniature Julius Caesar. This time, thank heaven, he was alone, and I tried to neutralize him with a mixture of charm and haughtiness.

The various couples had retired to their sleeping quarters and

I picked a room to share with Madame Adjouf, the wife of a big landowner in Morocco. She had an attractive, intelligent face with squirrel eyes, walked with her toes turned out, and was forever interrupting her tubby, sweet-natured, stammering husband—not that she often gave him a chance to stammer. I sent him off to join the three bachelors in their dormitory. Marquis Torti, to my relief, decided to sleep on the sofa in a huge room in which the four Italian women were installed.

'It's better than the Ritz here!' he yelped gaily.

As had happened in Omsk, the corridors had filled up as if by magic with four lines of beds between which I had to thread my way. There was scarcely a sound, just an occasional snore. All the Russian men were in their singlets; the women, buxom, full-bodied creatures, had taken off their blouses and were sleeping in their bras.

Tupolevs were soaring into the sky directly over our heads. I finally sank into a delightful sleep at five forty-five. At six o'clock I was woken up by screaming and shouting. It was time to get up. Haggard and bleary-eyed, I stumbled across the whole of snoring Siberia to get my flock out of bed. A delicious breakfast luxuriously served at the airport in delicate porcelain with shining cutlery restored our interest in life.

Soon after daybreak we were excitedly flying over Lake Baikal, which was sparkling between its chalky cliffs. I caught sight of a camp of painted felt tents called yurts belonging to Mongolian nomads. This was the only sign of life as far as the eye could see. The undulating countryside was covered with a sparse undergrowth powdered with snow.

I was beginning to feel scared. I had spent the last year reading books about China, and now I was on the threshold of a world of which I still knew nothing. Was I going to be able to enter that world and lead the way for my exacting flock?

# 3

For the moment, China and its hermetic existence took second place to an all-absorbing preoccupation: whom was I going to have to inform of the fact that his suitcase had gone astray somewhere in the vast spaces of Central Asia? General de Boilèle? God forbid. The painted vamp? Heaven help me.

Porters were emptying a flood of luggage into the huge tiled foyer of the Tsien Men Hotel, the Hotel of Friendship, where we had just arrived. Scattered here and there were a few tables dating back to about 1925. The walls were covered with brownish velvet hangings. On each table a huge thermos flask full of hot water sat in solitary splendour. On the right of the door was the reception desk. The receptionist spoke nothing but Chinese. How practical! On the left were the post office and the bank, where the clerks also spoke nothing but Chinese! As I gave each member of my party his room number I sent his luggage upstairs. Soon I was left in the foyer. Alone and utterly disconsolate: the missing suitcase was my own! My big black suitcase which had all my clothes inside! At the same time I found myself laughing with sheer relief. Half an hour later, in a hot bath, gazing at the dirty, crumpled suit I had worn since leaving Paris, now my only piece of clothing, I felt two huge tears rolling down my cheeks and disappearing into the bath-water.

My room was comfortable, even very comfortable. Writing paper, a cake of soap, a gigantic thermos flask full of hot water, the little canister of green tea which I was to find everywhere I went, and slippers at the foot of the bed. My window looked out on a little park in which two old women were strolling up and down. They were dressed in black tunics and trousers, their hair done in low chignons and their feet bound; and they were holding by the hand two tubby children in red and yellow who looked like comical peonies. Our first Chinese lunch went very quickly, which was very pleasant and, we found, the general rule. We were served at a long table in a huge dining-room by girls in blue cloth trousers and white blouses; some of them had long plaits hanging down their backs, while others wore their hair short. They were completely impassive, except when Pariet, our cultural guide, joked with them in Chinese. When that happened, their differences in character showed at once. One of them burst out laughing and became very friendly, another smiled but remained reserved, while a third pursed her lips and tried to ignore these uncivilized foreigners. The food was good and simple, a combination of European and Chinese dishes washed down with soda-water and a cool, light beer. The coffee, on the other hand, was an infusion of barley or something else. Torti and the Countess de Lissaye brought out their tins of Nescafé and called for hot water with a wealth of extravagant gestures. It was interesting to see how good food kept us happy, true Latins that we were. From being as strange as the planet Mars, China had suddenly become familiar and reassuring for us, thanks to a good meal.

In the afternoon we went on our first excursion in the city. We stopped for a moment in T'ien An Men Square, the Place de la Concorde of Peking which we had glimpsed that morning from the windows of our bus. Nowadays, in the huge, almost deserted square, there are only a few bicycles to be seen, an occasional lorry and one or two taxis, but everywhere traffic lights go on controlling a ghostly flow of bygone vehicles.

Children came trotting into the square, walking in groups of twenty under the guidance of girls in blue. Their full, rosy cheeks and smiling faces formed a curious contrast with the absolute silence they observed. They were dressed in blue trous-ers and brightly coloured smocks, and formed a double chain with each child holding the smock of the child in front. They looked like bunches of flowers on the wet pavements.

The rain stopped. We drove along broad avenues lined with single-storey houses covered with round grey tiles. At each corner the ridge-tile was turned upwards. Shin informed us that this traditional style had been abandoned in the construction of modern apartment houses because of the high cost involved.

'So there aren't any demons left in the new China?' sneered Noiret, the midget-emperor.

'Oh, yes, Monsieur Noiret, there are still some demons in

China, and Chairman Mao seems to have been having trouble with them lately. But I think he prefers to use more effective weapons against them than curved tiles!'

The sky was turning pink and I asked Shin to take us to the street of the antique-dealers. It was the end of the day and crowds of people were pouring out of the offices and workshops. The women were all dressed in the uniform blue cloth trousers and quilted greyish jackets, without the slightest coquetry in either their clothes or their bearing. Their faces were expressionless, their eyes far away. But they turned round behind our backs to look at us, and some of the younger ones burst out laughing at the sight of our shoes and stockings. The older ones went on their way impassively.

The men, on the other hand, didn't hesitate to meet our eyes and even to smile at us. They too were dressed in blue trousers, with matching tunics or warmer padded jackets. They all wore the same soft cap which made it impossible for us to tell them apart. Some of them were riding bicycles and rang their bells without stopping. Like the women they wore black felt slippers, and some of them had rubber ankle-boots. The street, like all the neighbouring streets, was spotlessly clean: there was not a single piece of paper or orange peel to be seen. I would notice the same thing everywhere: the whole of China seemed to have been swept clean a few minutes before we arrived.

My flock broke up, eaten up with curiosity. I went into a few little shops with wooden fronts, which were full of pretty porcelain and semi-precious statuettes of no great interest. I stopped in front of the window of a dealer in paintbrushes. Inside the shop, which was dimly lit by a single light-bulb hanging from the ceiling, I found a smiling middle-aged man. Seeing that I was interested in his brushes—he had all sorts, with waxed, varnished or lacquered wood, and hairs that were black or white, long or short—he put on for my benefit an extraordinary little ballet of paintbrushes against the background of the glass showcase. I was fascinated by the movements of the paintbrush characters: there was the slim, supple girl; the romantic young man; the stocky, broad-shouldered lout; the silent, white-haired old mother; and the sensible, dull-witted friend. It was the entire Peking Opera which was suddenly conjured up before my eyes with magical grace.

27

The antique-dealers of Peking are generally quite elderly. Most of them, Shin told us, used to own their shops. Now they are 'in partnership' with the government. They are not allowed to sell anything over a hundred years old. The price of their goods is fixed by a government agent who puts a red seal on each article which signifies that it has been 'approved as suitable for sale'.

Night had fallen and the narrow street was lit by only a few dim lights by the time we had all returned in a merry hubbub to our bus. Everybody unwrapped his minor purchases and major discoveries to show to the others. Sitting all alone at the back of the bus, I felt reasonably pleased with myself, slightly bewildered, and quite uncertain about what lay before us. I suggested to Shin that we should hold a conference on our return to the hotel to plan the rest of our stay in Peking in some detail.

Yuan, the gloomy, haughty-looking Chinese who had greeted us at the airport, led me ceremoniously into a thickly carpeted lounge on the fourth floor of the hotel which was furnished with a settee and several deep leather armchairs arranged in a semi-circle. In front of each armchair there was a low table set with tea, cigarettes, matches and an ashtray. The bust of Chairman Mao naturally presided over the discussion. Yuan trotted out an improved version of his speech at the airport, adding an expression of his admiration for my devotion to my task and begging me to spare him no criticism, for 'we have a great deal to learn from our French friends'. I began to suspect that this was going to be one of the chief themes of our journey and that all would go well provided that I never agreed to his request. I accordingly launched into a lyrical speech about the great Chinese people, my confidence in the success of our tour and my gratitude towards his friendly team.

Shin served us with tea, and we finally settled down to work. Yuan outlined the programme for our stay in Peking day by day, with Shin translating a sentence at a time. Yuan faced me while he was speaking in Chinese and looked at me when I answered in French as if we could understand each other. This gave me time to study him. The long face, the coarse features, the thick lips parted to reveal determination, and the perpetual smile which never lit up the eyes, betrayed a constant straining towards an aim which was never let out of sight. It was the face of a peasant, a man of action, a fanatic who knew no doubts. He was the perfect Party man.

Shin's translations were conscientious and rather brief. I wondered whether his knowledge of French was as extensive as it appeared. I would have to make myself clear and take care to correct any mistranslations. While he was talking I noticed his natural distinction and his eyes creased with merriment, concealed behind gold-rimmed glasses. He had a triangular, cat-like face and long, delicate hands; in other words the appearance of a bourgeois intellectual.

I was sitting on the settee on the left of Yuan, who had installed his staff on his right. I for my part had shy little Pariet on my left. To lend him added prestige in the eyes of the Chinese and to cement our relations, I kept leaning towards him and asking: 'What do you think, Jean?'

In an excited little voice he made a number of suggestions which were anything but stupid. He was charming, even touching. In Siberia he had been a good companion and a reliable colleague. He talked enthusiastically to the Chinese. He liked them already. His liberal heart and socialist mind made this journey a real mission for him. Would he be up to it? Yuan agreed to all our suggestions almost without discussion. We shook hands warmly, gazing into one another's eyes. 'Shee, shee.' 'Thank you, thank you.'

Back in my room I was relieved to find a little underwear sent to me by charming Colette Quesnel, the newspaper editor's widow, as well as some clothes, unfortunately too large for me, from Madame Blum and Madame Adjouf. The elegant Italian women, who were just my size, hadn't, alas, sent me so much as a handkerchief. Never mind! I was delighted with the underwear. I took a relaxing bath in the course of which I performed what was to become the daily ritual of doing my laundry. After which I gleefully made myself a cup of Nescafé, from a tin given to me by a friend who had known that I wouldn't find the Ritz in the land of Chairman Mao.

Our first dinner in Peking was at the Lacquered Duck, a restaurant on Tchien Men Wai Ta Thieh Avenue, a wide road lined with unlighted shops. Going through a large, brightly lit room in which a few foreigners were dining, we went into a private room and sat down at two round tables covered with white cloths. A well-trained head waiter in a white jacket promptly filled our large glass with cold beer and our two small glasses with mao-tai—rice alcohol—and a rather sweet warm red wine.

To my horror, Yuan stood up at the very beginning of the meal and launched out yet again into a speech on his usual themes: Franco-Chinese friendship, the lessons we could teach each other, and the friendly criticisms we should make of our hosts. After this homily he went round the room clutching his glass of mao-tai and clinked glasses with each guest in turn. When he had finished he shouted: 'Kampei!' and drained his glass at one gulp.

I in my turn stood up and, translated sentence by sentence by Shin, embarked on a pathetic flight of oratory on the same themes and proposed to my hilarious audience a 'Kampei' to Sino-French friendship. There then began the ritual of the Chinese meal: a dozen main dishes in rapid succession, surrounded by satellite dishes, variations often hard to define but always deliciously light—sharks' fins, salads, bamboo shoots, rotten eggs, roots, leaves, stalks, chicken and pork. Everything was lightly cooked and cut up into small pieces. The high spot of the evening was the arrival of the lacquered duck which was displayed to the company, taken away, and brought back cut up.

Lacquered with a paste of melted sugar, it had been filled with water and grilled on a wood fire, so that the outside was crisp while the inside remained tender. It was delicious. As an added treat we were given the duck's liver, a delicacy which would send our French gourmets into ecstasies. This feast was accompanied by a constant flow of mao-tai and red wine maintained by the vigilant head waiter, who never let our thimble glasses remain empty for more than a moment. As the guests' spirits rose, their voices grew louder. The Italians were particularly gay, and Torti kept fussing over his feminine neighbours. Noiret, whose nose had turned red, was extremely gracious to me. My little Swiss seemed to be in the seventh heaven of delight. Signora Leandri, who was taking on board huge shipments of mao-tai, professed to be delighted with the affectionate nickname of 'Grenadier' which I had found for her. Shin was not drinking and had started giving a slightly tipsy Pariet a somewhat involved lecture on Marxism. Shu on the other hand was drinking hard but remained as sober and silent as ever, her eyes creased in a constant effort of vigilance. As for Yuan, he was eating and drinking with obvious pleasure, conscious of the rarity of the occasion and the excellence of the fare.

The conversation was a little strained. It turned chiefly on a comparison of the climates of Peking and Paris, and of the rival merits of Chinese and French cooking. As soon as I asked a remotely personal question, Shin stopped translating while Yuan smiled at me uncomprehendingly. I told myself I must be patient. It was probably too soon for such questions.

Bowls of rice were brought in. Here we had to be careful, for courtesy forbade us to touch them. If we did, it would mean that the rich profusion of dishes which had been served had not been enough. I quickly passed round a warning *mezzo voce*.

Then Yuan brought the evening to an end after clearing his throat and spitting vigorously into his handkerchief, which he carefully put back into his pocket. My stomach turned over slightly and I whispered to Pariet the Sinophile:

'Is that customary here?'

'Of course,' he replied, with a touch of scorn for my bourgeois reaction. 'In every country in the Far East people clear their throats all the time.'

The meal turned out to be exceptionally cheap for our Western purses: ten francs each, or five yuans. As the average wage of a Peking worker was sixty yuans a month, it was obvious that a meal of that sort was a luxury the ordinary man or woman could seldom afford. I expressed my concern to Shu about all those dishes we had barely touched, in a country where every morsel of food was carefully counted. She replied without the slightest embarrassment that as soon as we had left, the staff of the restaurant would have flung themselves on our leavings like a flock of vultures. That allayed my thrifty bourgeois scruples.

We had all been given rooms together on the fifth floor of the hotel. A young porter handed us our keys—symbolic keys, since we should always find our doors open. Probably our Chinese hosts thought that the phrase 'the key to the door' was calculated to reassure their Western guests—and as politeness consists in assuring your guests of your good intentions, we had to be given keys of some sort. 'Their damned doors don't shut anyway,' snorted Adrienne Mandois. 'So what's the use of giving us keys?' But then, Madame Mandois had little use for symbols.

Before going upstairs, each member of my flock fought an individual battle to try to persuade the poor hall-porter to arrange for breakfast to be served next morning in his or her room. But as the time and nature of the order varied from one individualistic Latin to the next, I urged Pariet to clear things up for the perplexed porter. Appointing himself interpreter and scribe, he covered the poor man's notebook from right to left with graceful ideograms which had such prosaic meanings as 'Tea at eight o'clock for Room 543' or 'Coffee and rolls at 7.45 for Room 521'.

# 4

I opened one eye at six o'clock in the morning thanks to a concert of klaxons worthy of Paris in the days before sounding horns was forbidden.

It was already light outside—a dusty golden light—and I cursed the two cars responsible for the din. Swarms of cyclists were riding past, ringing their bells for all they were worth. A few red and blue buses drove by, packed with people. In the park behind the hotel, three girls in white blouses and black trousers were forcing a young man to get off his bicycle, roaring with laughter.

On this second morning in Peking I tried to get in touch with a French girl who was nearing the end of her second year as a student at Peking University. The Guimet Museum had told us that of all the French residents in Peking she knew the most about Chinese history and culture, and she had agreed to act as a lecturer and guide during our stay in the capital. Her name was Charlotte Florent.

At the other end of the line a metallic voice answered me curtly. There was a click, and we were cut off. I tried again. Another click. I went to look for Shin, who told me that I had to apply for permission to get in touch with a foreign student.

'Apply to whom?'

'I'll see to it myself.'

'I'd like to see the official who's responsible for giving permission,' I said.

'That official doesn't exist. I'll see to it myself.'

I took the opportunity to ask him to apply to the 'official who didn't exist' for permission to call on a Chinese doctor who had lived in England during the Second World War, when he had met one of my English friends.

Feeling sceptical about the results of my requests, I made

successive attempts to change some money and buy some post-cards and stamps. This all took a very long time. The young men at the *bureau de change* were earnest, silent and slow. The girls in pigtails who were selling postcards and stamps twittered like little birds and took out of a glass case a variety of stamps depicting flowers, landscapes, butterflies, peasants in the fields, factory scenes, dams under construction and craftsmen at work, as well as portraits of Chairman Mao and pictures of antiques, Chou bronzes and T'ang vases. Philately in China is a kaleido-scopic summary of national life. The girls handed over these little marvels as if they were gold coins, slowly and reluctantly. There was no gum on the backs of the stamps, nor on the flaps of the envelopes I bought—for reasons of hygiene, according to Shin, but possibly also for reasons of economy: you dipped a little brush into a pot of liquid gum and dabbed it on. The salesgirls worked out the price of my purchases on an abacus fitted with wooden balls like those we learned to count on at school. The rapid clicking of the balls delighted me. The abacus, I discovered, is the IBM computer of the Far East, and ardent propagandists maintain that a skilled operator can beat a computer hands down!

My next call was the telegraph office, where I sent off a few tearful cables in various directions in an attempt to find my suitcase. Georges Wolf, the gallery owner, was there, looking positively tragic and trying to send a cable to Paris. As with me, the girl at the counter conscientiously made him spell out every word in his cable. I felt my toes curling with impatience. Marquis Torti raised his voice to insist on his cable to Milan going express, while Adjouf timidly tried to attract the wander-ing attention of one of the cable-spellers. Finally we simply left a pile of unspelt telegrams on the counter to be sent off in our absence. The poor girls, bewildered by our noisy Latin exuber-ance, would have torn their hair out if such a dramatic gesture had been conceivable in China. It was five to nine and I started rounding up my group. Claude Adjouf, Madame Mandois and my dear Signora Leandri were missing. When Signora Leandri finally arrived, I gave a schoolmarmish frown and said sternly: 'You are five minutes late.' Then our vamp appeared on the horizon, wearing a golden yellow wig today, blood-red ski-pants and boots to match. We were all waiting for her in the coach and I took the opportunity to make a little speech.

34

'It's all right today. But from now on we start on the dot, and I shall assume that anybody who isn't here doesn't want to come on the excursion.'

In the sharp, crystal air of the Peking autumn we felt happy and excited as we came to the beautiful T'ien An Men Square we had glimpsed the day before. Now the centre of the capital, it used to be just the entrance to the Forbidden City, a name changed by Mao to that of the Imperial City, which refers to the succession of courtyards, audience chambers and palaces to which entry was forbidden in the past, under pain of death, to anyone who was not in the Emperor's suite.

The gilded pavilion from which Mao harangues the crowds on public holidays guards the road leading to the Palace. We crossed the canal by an arched marble bridge with carved balustrades and entered the first courtyard, flanked on the north by the first pavilion. The sight took our breath away. The huge courtyard was so to speak crisscrossed with white marble balustrades bristling with cylinders of the same material. The proportions were beautiful and the whole courtyard, which sloped gently up towards the pavilion, looked as if it were moving. On either side of the entrance to the pavilion, bronze dragons eight feet high looked down on children who were spending their day off school sweeping the outer courtyards with long-handled triangular straw brooms. This was how the authorities hoped to rid the minds of the young of the bourgeois revisionist idea that intellectual work was superior to manual labour. It was in accordance with the same principle, Shin told me, that students spent their annual holidays in the fields or in a factory. Shin privately admitted to me that he preferred the country because of the fresh air, but said that he thought that he would probably have to go into a factory the following year. In the same way, doctors, high-ranking officers and leading officials of the régime periodically made an effort—or were obliged to make an effort —to 'regain contact with the masses', to avoid the creation of a new class consciousness. Several years before, Chairman Mao himself had been seen throwing a few pebbles on to the site of a new dam.

On the left of the courtyard I discovered to my surprise a plot of what looked like fresh green grass, nine feet square. The grass turned out to be wheat, and the patch, I learned, was the caretaker's private plot, the produce from which he was entitled to eat or sell, at the official price of course. A little farther on, other schoolchildren were pulling up the grass growing between the paving stones. The pavilion shone brightly in the morning sunshine with its lofty roof with its projecting edges and turned-up corners. It was covered with gilded tiles, all round and shining, and supported by bare wooden columns with brick walls in the spaces in between.

The whole building was painted red. 'It's symbolic,' sighed Signora Leandri, her ample bosom heaving like a pair of black-smith's bellows. Dear Signora Leandri, the red paint had noth-ing to do with the colour of the régime: the enemies of the building were not revisionists but ants and rainstorms. We went into the pavilion and in the middle found a huge statue of Buddha in gilded stucco watched over by grimacing figures of guardians standing against the side walls under a beamed, multi-coloured ceiling.

A silent crowd moved through the building: women holding peony-children by the hand, a few soldiers wearing their usual unattractive soft caps, and an ivory-faced old man with a pointed beard. They examined us with impassive curiosity.

I kept searching the horizon in the direction of T'ien An Men Square. Where the devil had Pariet got to? Why wasn't he here to give his little lecture? We were all gathered round that horrible Buddha waiting for him. At last he arrived, running across the courtyard, a pale, breathless figure. For some reason he was carrying an overcoat, a camera, and a packet of films.

'Where the hell have you been? Hurry up—we've all been waiting for you.'

'General de Boilèle says we're going too fast for him,' he groaned. 'He's at the main entrance and he refuses to budge until you come and fetch him yourself. He insisted on my carry-ing his coat. He asked Shu to carry it first but she replied that she wasn't a porter.'

Poor Pariet's eyes were shining with tears of exasperation.

'You aren't a porter either as far as I know. I think the best thing to do would be to dump all that stuff on this little wall in the sunshine and give us the benefit of your knowledge of the Imperial City.'

For three hours we walked through almost identical court-yards and pavilions, all built along the same north-south axis so that the Emperor should always be able to face south during an audience. The ridge-tiles, bristling with dragons, soldiers, riders and fishes at every curve of the roof, stood out like gold statuettes against the bright blue sky.

My Sinologist was a disappointment. Pariet trotted out a few commonplace little lectures, in a monotonous voice with a staccato delivery. It was all terribly dull, an uninspiring collection of dates and unadorned facts. He was obviously afraid of annoying our Chinese guides, who were supposed to give us an explanatory lecture themselves, but who were clearly incapable of telling us anything except that it was thanks to the People's efforts that the Imperial City had been built, and that it had now reverted to the People. I tugged at Pariet's sleeve and murmured:

'For heaven's sake give them some anecdotes, some details, some life!'

Pariet's fears appeared to be completely superfluous. The Chinese didn't seem at all annoyed and eagerly noted down every word he spoke, which led me to suspect that they knew even less than he did.

But this was not the end of my worries, for all of a sudden Adrienne Mandois drew me to one side. Pursing her thick, crudely painted lips, and fluttering her eyelashes as if she were acting in a melodrama, she informed me that she was suffering from 'an intestinal disorder', that she wanted to see the Embassy doctor 'and not one of those Chinese quacks', and finally that it was obviously 'the fault of that damned lacquered duck'. I deposited her on another little wall in the sunshine, thinking to myself that before long every wall in the Imperial City would bear some trace of our visit.

In spite of obstacles and interruptions, we finally reached the Imperial apartments. Here we found some handsome lacquered furniture, some Chinese bronzes and porcelains, and a few European bronzes of no great interest. Repeatedly destroyed by fire and then rebuilt, the apartments conjured up none of those moving memories which haunt our European palaces. This palace had been occupied only by a succession of more or less ridiculous princes whose names were lost in the cruel night of Chinese history.

Silent and sombre as an Imperial dragon, the General arrived at last, accompanied by the beautiful Madame Trollan. Scorning his wrath, I shepherded my flock into the Museum of the Imperial Palace. A huge genealogical tree greeted us at the

37

entrance: starting from a fish, the trunk and branches ended up in the figure of a worker in dungarees. The Museum was crowded with portraits and statues of the Emperors of China, Che Huang Ti, Kublai Khan and Confucius, Han bronzes, T'ang pottery, and wonderful Sung paintings on an old gold ground, round-shaped so that they could be used for fans. Bunches of schoolchildren stood gazing silently at the showcases. As we came out into the first courtyard of the Palace, a group of men and women lined up in three files fifty yards long rocked with laughter at the sight of us. This unexpected display of hilarity produced very different reactions among my flock. Amusement in pretty Isabella, my little Swiss and a few others. Obvious annoyance in General de Boilèle and Madame Mandois, who asked with a frown: 'What are they laughing at? They're the ones that look peculiar.' As for my Sinologist, he whispered unhappily in my ear:

'This is impossible. I can't stand a whole month of it.'

The failings of my cultural adviser incited me to launch a fresh offensive. I insisted on Shin putting me in touch with that young Frenchwoman who lived in Peking. After this preliminary venture into the mysteries of China's complicated history, she had become a sort of lifebuoy in my eyes. She alone could show us Peking and its treasures.

Shin finally handed me the receiver: at the other end of the line I heard to my relief the French voice I had been expecting. She would be with me in an hour.

I had no sooner hung up than I was pounced on by the groaning Mandois who had spent the entire morning stuck to her little wall like a limpet to a rock. I pushed her into a taxi which Shu sent off to the French Embassy in search of a miracle-working doctor with a cure for defective intestines.

Wrapping up my request in all the blandness I could muster, I asked Yuan to send a cable to Moscow about my missing suitcase. In order to obtain this favour, I slowly expressed my appreciation of his efforts in a long, involved compliment. Then, after receiving a reply in the same style, I repeated what I had said, expressing a very similar idea in completely different terms. All this took a good twenty minutes, but it provided me with excellent training in mental agility and self-control.

Completely beige, from her shoes to her short hair, the Messiah finally arrived, in the person of Charlotte Florent, the young

Frenchwoman whose learning, I hoped, was going to make up for the deficiencies of my home-grown Sinologist. Off we went to the History Museum, one of the two monumental edifices which flank T'ien An Men Square, a huge white building with square columns and flat roofs in the style of the Twenties. A succession of vast halls paved in marble and lined with show-cases awaited us. We began with the Stone Age. Charlotte managed very well. Rather shy to begin with, she soon got into her stride. She was precise, eloquent and interesting. Tremend-ously relieved, I smiled happily at Pariet as he came hurrying towards me.

'Yuan wants to see you straight away,' he said. 'He's furious about Charlotte Florent showing you over the Museum.'

My heart beating wildly, I waited for Yuan to come to me. Shin looked annoyed and Shu's face was as blank as a brick wall.

An expressionless Yuan advanced upon me slowly.

'You were given permission to telephone Madame Florent,' he declared, 'but not to engage her to give lectures.'

'This was all arranged several months ago,' I replied calmly. 'Madame Florent asked for permission through the French Em-bassy.'

'Madame Florent is a student at Peking University and her studies leave her no time to devote to other activities.'

'You must be mistaken,' I retorted, 'seeing that she is here.'

This was a blunder on my part. Stating an obvious fact is sheer folly in China. There, obvious facts lose their factual quality, and even more their obviousness. What is more, irony is a form of expression which is not understood in China, or worse still, misunderstood.

'Madame Florent,' Yuan said stubbornly, 'has not been given permission either to give you lectures or to act as a guide. As a matter of courtesy, however, you may continue the present tour, but that is all.'

'Madame Florent is a friend of mine,' I said. 'I should like to invite her to dinner this evening.'

'What you do this evening lies outside our programme. So you may do what you like.'

'Thank you, Monsieur Yuan,' I said, 'for your co-operation and understanding.'

Yuan's smile, which hadn't altered one iota during our argument, vanished like an oyster closing. All the same he added:

39

'I would like to tell you how much I appreciate your collaboration and to say once more how useful any contact with our foreign friends is for us.'

Charlotte had not noticed what was happening. Warming to her subject and gaining in confidence, she was speaking more loudly now and keeping her audience enthralled. She described the long history of the Imperial dynasties, which was illustrated in the Museum by a remarkable series of models. Yuan suddenly intervened. Speaking in short, naïve, staccato sentences, he attacked the feudal slavery of Imperial China, went on to con-demn the slavery of the colonial period, and finished up with the usual denunciation of the after-effects of these successive slaveries which the young people of China should try to eradicate for ever. Within a few seconds we had passed from the mysteries of History to the certainties of the Cultural Revolution.

Room after room with walls covered with photographs show-ing Mao and his followers during the heroic era of the Long March illustrated the modern period of Chinese history. Under each photograph a large inscribed panel provided explanations in schoolroom language. Yuan kept adding his grain of salt, prophesying that the Chinese Revolution would rapidly spread to all parts of the world, notably Africa and Latin America, and declaring that it was the miracle of the modern world. To my horror he turned to me and asked me to confirm what he had just said. My heart sank as I saw my companions' sarcastic smiles. What was I to do? Taking my courage in both hands, I launched into a few statements of the most consummate jesuitry:

'Yes, the Revolution is a miracle, but ... a purely Chinese miracle, since the Chinese are one of the most courageous, hard-working, long-suffering peoples in the whole world ... I doubt whether a similar miracle could take place in the steaming tropics of Africa or Latin America ...'

Shin translated what I had said. Yuan looked perplexed, even annoyed. He took out his little black notebook and scribbled something in it.

Poor Yuan. He was at once touching and irritating with his cast-iron faith, his conviction that he possessed absolute truth. And in spite of the traps and obstacles he kept putting in my path, I took care not to oppose him in any way.

A little later, on the way to the Museum of the Revolution,

a building in the Stalin style which houses the relics of the revolutionary struggle, I myself harangued my pilgrims, trying to kindle in their cold, even hostile eyes something of the heroic fire of the Long March and to bring them closer to that great drama of the Chinese revolution.

I told them of the Chinese communists concentrated in Southern China, mostly peasants and all volunteers who had fought a harsh guerrilla war since 1928.

In 1930, Chiang Kai-shek had started a war of extermination against them and had launched four tough offensives. The German communist general, Li Teh (Otto), smuggled into China by the Russian Komintern, was in favour of a defensive war, against the advice of Mao Tse-tung and Chu Teh, the communist leaders. As a result the communists lost control of the cities they were defending and suffered tremendous casualties.

At this point the Red leaders made a dramatic decision: they gave up their small, soviet republic in the south, took what men they had left, roughly ninety thousand, leaving behind about ten thousand partisans for a rearguard action and, on October 16, 1934 began one of the greatest strategic retreats in the history of mankind.

The Red army loaded animals and bearers with all the equipment and food it could muster and then crossed Southern China from east to west, turning north along the Tibetan mountains. They marched through deserts, marshes, ravines, passes, climbed snow-topped mountains thirteen thousand feet high, camped in soaking forests in pouring rain and for most of the time suffered appalling hardship without food, water, medicines and clothing.

From then on Mao was virtually recognized as the Commander of the campaign. He imposed a strict discipline on his troops in their relations with the local populations: no raping, no stealing, no pillaging. He formulated eight rules for the troops which they sang as they marched:

1 Put the doors back in place when leaving a house (the doors, being very light, were used as bedding).
2 Roll up your mat and give it back.
3 Be polite and helpful to people.
4 Give back every item you have borrowed.
5 Replace all damaged items.

6 Be honest with the peasants.

7 Pay for everything you buy.

8 Respect rules of hygiene and fix up latrines at a decent distance from houses.

Of course, the strict rules combined with the incredible hardship involved led to numerous desertions. Many of the enthusiastic young men who went through the ordeal died during the constant fighting they had to endure against the harrying troops of Chiang Kai-shek. It was at this time that Mao established once and for all the tactics of guerrilla warfare:

1 When the enemy advances, withdraw.

2 When the enemy stops to camp, harry him.

3 When the enemy avoids fighting, attack.

4 When the enemy withdraws, run after him.

The strong point of Mao's political tactics was, by good behaviour and political education to win over the populations the Reds met during their march and convert them to communism. So that, having left the Kiangsi province in the South and reached Yenan in the Shensi province in the West, they had established, in spite of the fact that there were only 30,000 volunteers left, a Red zone right across China which was to provide the communists with a strong and reliable base upon which they would build their future.

The survivors had had their education too. While walking over six thousand miles, twice the distance from the east coast to the west coast of America, one behind the other, those illiterate peasants had learnt to read. The man in front wore on his back a piece of cloth upon which was painted a sign of the Chinese alphabet. The man immediately behind had plenty of time in which to memorize the sign. When he had learnt it, they would change places in the marching line and each would have a new sign to contemplate and remember. The Chinese are one of the brightest people in the world.

It took them an entire year to get to Yenan and to master the two thousand commonly used signs in the Chinese alphabet. They had survived, achieved a gigantic feat and laid the foundation of the future Red administration.

Madame Chapeau, Laure de Castillat, Colette, the Adjoufs

and the Musketeers were perfectly ready to thrill to the tale of this Shakespearian epic. Besides, they knew at least as much about the subject as I did. But some of the others assumed frosty expressions. After hearing an account of the incredible sufferings endured by the heroes of the Long March, Signora Coli pursed her perfect lips and murmured: 'They didn't have to do it,' taking my breath away. Her neighbour, the Peruvian Madame Neralinda, went one better, remarking: 'Yes, they did, the poor things: they were terrorized into doing it.'

I was appalled by the realization of my inability to touch the imagination of these people, my fellow Europeans, who were just as blindly attached to their beliefs as Yuan. I would have liked to see them silent, respectful, and deeply moved by this story of courage, heroism, cold, hunger, fear and suffering which I had just told as best I could, though doubtless rather clumsily.

For a moment I felt utterly discouraged, insignificant little woman that I was in the face of this vast country which I already found deeply moving, and which I was trying to absorb through every pore of my being and to offer to these people who had made the effort of coming here, but who for the most part were incapable of abandoning their preconceived ideas and established opinions.

A rat-faced, pimply young man greeted us at the main door. Brandishing a long pointer, he led us at a fair trot past more photographs of Mao and Chu Teh at the time of the Long March. Other photographs showed soldiers of the famous Eighth Army and group portraits of the first revolutionary government. Our progress was accompanied by a monotonous commentary given in a shrill little voice. In the middle of the last hall a huge map lit up on our arrival which showed the courses taken by the various armies on the Long March, together with the dates of their exploits. It was fascinating. Signora Negri, who clearly did not know that only a tenth of the three hundred thousand men who for a whole year had fought their way back across six thousand miles, in conditions of terrible hardship, through the bleakest regions in the world, had finally reached Yenan, asked:

'How many men reached their destination?'

'A hundred thousand,' our rat-faced guide replied smartly.

My heart missed a beat, and nearly stopped altogether when the same guide admitted that he didn't know the arrival point of the Long March. I placed myself at the service of Chairman Mao, even at the risk of making our comrade-guide lose face. I was astounded that the younger generation, the generation which had known neither the colonial occupation nor the Chiang Kai-shek régime, and which was entirely a product of the present régime, did not know the history of the Revolution, and above all one of the greatest epics of mankind, an epic which had taken place only yesterday.

We trailed about for another hour. I left the Museum in a fury, feeling that this visit, which should have filled us all with enthusiasm, whatever our personal opinions, had been just a monotonous routine lecture.

My anger, and the courage of the three hundred thousand Chinese who had been on the Long March, gave me the boldness to confront Yuan in the hotel foyer.

'Are you or aren't you going to let me meet an official of Luxingsche?' I asked. (Luxingsche is the name of the Government tourist agency.)

Yuan remained silent at first, and then replied:

'I don't think so, because I am the person responsible for everything that concerns your group. So it's to me that you must say anything you wish to say to Luxingsche.'

I flared up at this.

'Well, I've got lots of things to say to Luxingsche, Monsieur Yuan, and I'll tell you a few of them now.'

Laure and Colette, who were hanging about nearby, drew nearer, pricking up their ears. The Musketeers watched the scene open-mouthed. For my part I felt ready to take on single-handed Chiang Kai-shek, the Japanese, anybody and everybody.

'Listen, Monsieur Yuan: we have an enormous admiration for all that your country has achieved in less than twenty years. But you keep asking me for criticisms with praiseworthy persistence. Well, here's one to be getting on with ...'

Shin was quite pale. Shu had wrinkled her forehead and her nose, and pursed her lips. The three Chinese were standing all around me. I felt as comfortable as if I had been in the middle of a rugby scrum.

'Will you kindly explain to me,' I went on, 'why you refuse to allow me the help of a woman of the calibre of Charlotte Florent, who has proved her admiration for the People's Republic by devoting two years of her life to studying it, when all that you can find to give me as a guide is an almost illiterate young man, just about fit to talk to primary school children but certainly not to people who know the history of the Chinese Revolution as well as their own.'

Anyone would have thought that lightning had struck the foyer. Laure and Colette were petrified. The Musketeers were still open-mouthed. I turned on my heel and walked with dignity towards the restaurant where Shin caught up with me.

'You will have your answer this afternoon,' he said.

At the dinner table I was spoken to with a certain respect, as if the Long March had been nothing but a weekend jaunt compared with the battle I had just fought. The Musketeers chuckled delightedly over it. Only Adrienne remained impassive, waiting until dessert before giving me the latest news of her intestinal disorders. She was still wearing her ski-pants and red boots, and her wig was beginning to look a little greasy.

# 5

I broke the bad news to Charlotte Florent, giving her an account of my tussle with Yuan.

'The fools! The cretins!' she roared. 'They'll never learn! I don't give a damn—I'm staying with you!'

Lost in admiration at this vigorous reaction, I nonetheless remained obsessed with the idea that some microphones might be hidden under the carpet or behind the bed, and I urged my compatriot to be more cautious.

'Dear Charlotte,' I said, 'two days in China have already taught me the futility of losing my temper. Naturally we would prefer to discover Peking with you who know it so well, rather than with poor little Pariet. But you know better than I do that if we insisted on having you as our guide, the Chinese would be sure to put us on the first plane back to Europe, and to expel you from the University and possibly from China. It's obvious that the Chinese have no desire to let us mix with foreign students, possibly to prevent any alteration of a certain image of their country which they try to present to tourists. Don't you think that's the reason?'

My words left Charlotte cold, and she went on fulminating against 'the stupidity of the Chinese'. You might just as well try to make pigs fly, I said to myself, still thinking of hidden microphones. I finally stopped the flow by inviting her to share our dinner, during which she could give us a lecture on the history of Peking, as the Chinese wouldn't be present at the meal. Coming out of my room, I bumped into two members of the hotel staff standing outside my door, which was obviously an easier method of listening to conversations than microphones.

After dinner Pariet broke down and poured his heart out to me. Everything came out, notably his disappointment in the face of the hardness of the Chinese, for the poor, idealistic man had formed a wonderful idea of what they would be like. He realized too that he wasn't cut out to be a guide, that he was doing his job badly, and that the obtuseness and pretentiousness of my companions horrified him. He knew that he was throwing the whole burden of the journey on to me and he humbly begged me to forgive him. In short he had a good cry on my shoulder. I comforted him with motherly advice, words of affection, and a tranquillizer which I said was a vitamin pill.

While I was in the foyer trying to send off my umpteenth cable to Aeroflot begging them to find my suitcase, I ran into my little Swiss. He was really the funniest, most delightful companion anyone could wish for. His jokes, related in a deadpan Genevese voice, always sent me into convulsions. But for the moment he was convulsed with laughter himself. He had wanted to find out whether it was true what people said, namely that in communist countries your luggage was searched. He had stuck sellotape on both his suitcases before going out. Well, on his return the sellotape had been pulled off both cases.

'That proves, doesn't it, my dear Madame, that what they say is true?'

Georges Wolf then appeared on the scene, pointing a packet of postcards at me like a bayonet. Isabella, it turned out, had asked him to post them for her.

'These are dynamite!' he exclaimed in a tragic tone of voice. 'The girl's mad!'

I shamelessly started reading them.

'Here,' she had written, 'people live in a state of terror. That is why they dare not rebel. They follow the Party line because it is impossible for them to do anything else...'

All this was not even concealed inside the illusory cover of an envelope. All that we needed was trouble with the censorship! In front of my two bewildered friends I tore up the cards and put the pieces in my handbag: after all, you never know. Dear Isabella, don't blame the Chinese Post Office, which does its job very well, and forgive me.

# 6

The Temple of Heaven looked very peaceful, with its dark blue tiles shining in the sun, its broad terraces, and the golden light of a Peking afternoon.

Yuan was smiling blandly, the others strolling about, laughing and talking. They were in a gay mood, and the atmosphere was very light-hearted. Boilèle was smiling. The Mandois woman was scratching herself. Dupont was joking with Isabella, but the way he was looking at her told me that the feelings of my little Swiss were becoming more serious than they seemed. 'Careful,' I thought, 'you are no match for that beautiful girl, who may be very nice but is also spoilt and coquettish.' Some of our group were taking films, and others chatting on a little wall in the sunshine. In one of the courtyards two boys and two girls were playing with a skipping-rope. Dupont joined in, followed by Isabella, the Adjoufs and me. The Chinese children laughed and clapped their hands. Together we organized some little games, and we were joined by a few soldiers from a neighbouring camp. All of a sudden, in front of the Temple of Heaven, East and West were fraternizing by playing children's games together. A few weeks later, not far from that spot, a howling mob would lay siege to the French Embassy.

Here the Emperor came once a year to thank the gods for the benefits conferred on the country during the previous year, the last Emperor to perform this ritual being Yuan Shih-kai in 1912. The Temple of Heaven owes its name to its shape and colour: it is 'as round and blue as heaven'. Struck by lightning and burnt to the ground in 1889, it was completely rebuilt with rare timber imported from the United States, a fact which for some reason sent Adrienne Mandois into a fit of sniggering. Simone de Beauvoir once compared this temple in a happy phrase to 'a half-opened blue umbrella'. After playing for a while in the Courtyard of the Echo, we climbed the so-called 'Charcoal Hill', a huge mound made of earth extracted from the artificial lakes. On this mound, from which we could see Peking turning pink in the light of the setting sun, Li the Brave, the last of the Ming Emperors, hanged himself in 1664 after a military defeat. Before dying, Li wrote on the lining of his garment: 'A weak man of little virtue, I have offended the Gods, and the rebels have captured my capital ... Ashamed of appearing before my ancestors, I am about to die.' Emperor Li may be said to have invented autocriticism ...

Coming down the tree-shaded steps on the hillside, I asked Shin, for whom I felt a certain liking, why the People's Government continued to maintain and open to the public the monuments of Imperial China and the China of the colonial era. Was their artistic value regarded as more important than political considerations? He looked embarrassed, hesitated for a moment, hurried off to consult Yuan, and came back to tell me:

'It isn't to revive a past we hate that we keep these mementoes, but to show our foreign visitors and our own people things which are the work of the Chinese people and therefore their property.'

From the top of the hill I had noticed a large pagoda. As we were passing it I asked Shin to stop our coach. Our guide didn't seem to like the idea. The building had once been a Buddhist shrine erected by the first Manchu Emperor, and stood like a gigantic sugar-loaf in the middle of a vast courtyard surrounded by a row of wretched huts. Out of these huts poured a horde of women in patched clothes and children who were rather grubby but happy and obviously healthy. In spite of gigantic efforts, I discovered later, education was not yet universal in China, and when children did not go to school their mother had to stay at home to look after them, with the result that the family had only one wage-earner and sank into greater poverty. In front of each hut there was a little stove which burnt wood and coal, and which served as both cooker and radiator. The children crowded round us but Yuan refused to let us go into the courtyard and said something to the children who drew back. This was our first contact with the China of the Chinese, the China that lived a precarious tight-rope existence. I looked around me. What I saw was poor, even very poor, but it was neither dirty nor depressing, possibly because of the gaiety of the children. There was nothing here of the poverty and sadness of India. Here nobody had the tragic hollow-eyed look of undernourishment. Signora Negri started filming the scene. Yuan tried to stop her, on the ground that nobody had the right to film other people without their permission. But the children were so fascinated that they all began tugging at the Italian woman's coat to look into the lens of her camera.

An exasperated Yuan hustled us back into our coach. Once we were inside, Shin told me:

'There will be a conference on the fourth floor at 5.10.'

The precise timing of this conference surprised me.

'You're sure it's at 5.10, Shin, not 5.12?'

He looked at me in astonishment and a smile slowly rose from the depths of this serious, conscientious young man. I could almost see this smile making its way through the successive layers of Party loyalty, devotion to the principle of collectivity, and admiration for Chairman Mao. Up and up it came, and finally it emerged, creasing his eyes without touching his mouth, so that it acquired a secretive, even conspiratorial quality. Dear Shin had no sense of humour. It was not that my question had been terribly funny, but my little Chinese was so obviously a man of absolute faith and self-righteousness. Shu for her part oscillated between peevishness and a sense of fun. Her faith, or rather her virtue, struck me as less rigid than Shin's.

At exactly ten minutes past five, smiling broadly, I entered the fourth-floor conference room, followed by Pariet. The Chinese had been waiting for us for two minutes and were sitting in the same places as the first day. A waiter in a white jacket served tea and then withdrew. I lit a cigarette, a Kent bought at Le Bourget, with a match pulled out of a book given by the Sheraton Park Hotel in Washington. The funny side of the situation made me smile to myself and helped me to relax. I still felt a certain anxiety as I waited to hear what Yuan had to say to me. He began by clearing his throat and spitting ceremoniously. Then he started speaking in a slow, low voice, gazing at me intently all the time with his slanting eyes and his unchanging smile. He went on, damn him, on and on. Feeling vaguely uneasy, I drew on my cigarette to keep face. Shin was looking rather embarrassed. What could Yuan be saying? At long last he stopped. Shin stood up, pulled his chair over to my sofa, and opened fire.

'I think,' he declared, 'that there is a serious misunderstanding between us. Naturally everything isn't perfect in China. There are many things which remain to be done. But before the Liberation we had nothing. Nonetheless we took a great deal of time and trouble preparing for the visit of our distinguished guests. We think we have received you in a friendly fashion and to the best of our ability, and hope that you are satisfied with your accommodation. That is why it is all the more distressing for us to discover that you are angry about the incident with Madame Florent and that you consider our guides inadequate. We understand that perfectly, but as we cannot offer you any better guides we would quite understand if you decided not to continue your journey and left China tomorrow, for example.'

Shin was suffering. Yuan smiled. Shu didn't bat an eyelid. Pariet was choking. I lit another cigarette with a Sheraton match. I offered one to Yuan who asked me if my cigarettes were French. 'No,' I said, without any further comment. I lit it for him with another match from the Sheraton. You could have heard a pin drop. Thanks to the matches I regained some of my composure. I tried to think fast. What made my task all the harder was the fact that I thought the man was perfectly right. It was true that they had come a terribly long way, and that what they were offering us was amazing for them, and would have done credit to any fully developed nation. It was true that we were blasé, capricious visitors, ungrateful and perpetually dissatisfied. I felt considerable sympathy for this man who had gone to enormous trouble, believed in what he was doing, and didn't hesitate to burn his bridges when the other side asked too much. I even felt strongly tempted to tell him of the respect and admiration I felt for him. But this time not in order to obtain a favour—this wasn't the time for that. We were playing a game, and something more serious than ping-pong.

'As you say, Monsieur Yuan, a terrible misunderstanding has arisen between us. If you haven't noticed our gratitude for your welcome and our admiration for your achievements, then a misunderstanding has certainly come between us. What is more, if you haven't realized that I am all too conscious of the courtesy I owe your country and the responsibility I have assumed towards my group even to consider leaving China a day before the date set for our departure, then a serious misunderstanding has occurred. Now please help me to understand this: why do you refuse

51

to allow us to enjoy Madame Florent's co-operation? Has she behaved badly in any way? I beg you to be completely frank with me.'

Yuan replied at length, smiling all the time and without batting an eyelid.

'Your request cannot possibly be granted. Madame Florent is a student at Peking University and her curriculum doesn't allow her time to engage in other activities, even for a few days. I would like to tell you how much I admire your hard work and your sense of responsibility and how happy we are to welcome your group. We realize that we are unworthy of receiving such distinguished visitors and that we have a great deal to learn from our French friends.'

I started wriggling uncomfortably on the sofa.

'No, no,' I protested.

'But we do,' insisted Yuan. 'What is more, we regard your criticisms as a token of friendship. We are in the process of forming strong bonds of friendship between our two countries, and it is our duty to strengthen them even further.'

I thought of the remarks about China made by Adrienne Mandois and other members of my party, and this praise of our 'criticisms' cut me to the quick. But I banished these thoughts in order to exert all the charm I could. And I was grateful to him for the escape hatch he was offering me, knowing that there was nothing left for me to do but jump through it.

'Dear Monsieur Yuan,' I said, 'I appreciate enormously your generous words and in order to prove to you the strength of the bonds between us I am going to give you proof of our friendship: I am ready to abandon Madame Florent's co-operation. In return I presume that you will do your best to make things easy for us on our journey.'

Yuan had enough tact not to look as if he regarded my renunciation of Madame Florent's co-operation as a victory for himself. He stood up abruptly, followed by Shin and Shu, and shook both my hands vigorously. 'No more misunderstandings!' sighed Shin. I too stood up, shook hands all round, expressed my thanks, and walked out with all the majesty I could muster, leaving the Sheraton matches on the table.

We dined early and rapidly, a simple matter thanks to the speedy and increasingly smiling service we were given at the hotel. For we were going to the Opera, and the performance was due to begin at half-past seven. The theatre was packed to the doors when we arrived. The walls were bare, and the wooden seats made a tremendous clatter as we put them down. The performance began, with the text projected in Chinese script on a luminous screen on each side of the stage.

The show was a very popular modern opera entitled *The Women's Squad of the Red Army*. During the rest of our stay we were to see nothing but plays and modern operas with patriotic themes, such as the Japanese War or the struggle against Chiang Kai-shek's troops. The old operas with their fabulous costumes dripping with embroidery and gold braid had been banned some time before. The Ministry of Culture considered that stories about Emperors and concubines were not suitable subjects for a popular art capable of being understood by the masses, made no contribution to the advance of communism, and did nothing to destroy the roots of revisionism and the bourgeois spirit. The workers and above all the peasants of China, uneducated as most of them were, needed an art which was intelligible and therefore extremely simple.

The curtain rose without any warning to reveal a set representing the home of a rich landowner. Powerless to help, we witnessed the calvary of a pretty girl who was beaten and pricked with a hairpin by the landowner's wife. Fortunately her sufferings and ours did not last long. Revolting against the landlord's cowardly and brutal attempts to seduce her, our heroine fled into the mountains, where by a providential chance she met a band of guerrillas. These guerrillas turned out to be women: one of the famous women's squads of the Red Army. They made our heroine welcome, comforted her, emancipated her, and trained her in guerrilla warfare, dressed her in attractive bermuda shorts and a no less attractive cap. The delighted audience wriggled happily in their seats, laughing and giggling. But nobody clapped.

After an interval during which we were kept at a distance from the rest of the audience, the curtain rose again on a tropical set of rivers and palm-trees in which partisans were learning to shoot by firing at a wooden effigy of Chiang Kai-shek. Inspired by revolutionary zeal, our heroine now proceeded to make a monumental blunder. She started a fight which turned out badly for the guerrillas. But she did her autocriticism and was given another chance. A little re-education and everything turned out well; she returned to the fold. So much for individualism, even when it was well-meant...

The curtain fell on a grand finale with a feminine choir dressed in khaki singing underneath a fluttering red flag. The dancers were graceful and pretty, especially in the pre-revolutionary scenes in which they wore silk dresses. Their femininity was much less obvious in the scenes where they were dressed in uniform. The choreography was Western in style and rather sweet and simple, with Soviet influence showing in a dance of partisans. Something of the old Chinese tradition was still discernible in the somewhat feline grace of the movements.

The contrast between the women on the stage and those in the audience was extremely striking. The latter looked dull and uninteresting, and wore clothing rather than clothes. There was no make-up on their faces, their hair-style was a uniform basin-crop, and their general appearance was devoid of coquetry and even femininity. The girls on the stage, on the other hand, wore face-powder, and their lips and cheeks were rouged. Their bodies were delicate, their gestures lively and graceful, their costumes rich and silky. Actors, acrobats and dancers are picked out at primary school, receive a special training, and form a privileged class which enjoys a far higher standard of living than the rest of the population, They alone are allowed access to high-quality clothes and cosmetics, which are regarded as luxury goods in this country where a large part of the population still lacks the basic necessities. It was obvious that the poor working-class women who made up the greater part of the feminine element of the audience had neither the time nor the money to think about their femininity. Moreover, the Spartan virtues preached by the new régime clearly discouraged both coquetry and flirtation, a fact which seemed to distress some of my companions. Noiret uttered a series of frustrated clucking noises at the sight of the dancers, and nudged a hilarious Dupont in the ribs. Marquis Torti declared that he found 'these little Chinese girls absolutely charming', and Monsieur Blum radiated joy, while a gloomy-looking Wolf criticized the choreography. As for Mandois, she kept shrugging her shoulders in scorn, convinced that 'in Paris they would be hissed off the stage'.

In the third act, unable to stand all this any longer, I went to sit next to Shin to listen in peace to his translation of the libretto, a literal translation which he gave me in a stentorian bellow. Nobody around us made the slightest objection. Feeling slightly embarrassed, I thought how exasperated I was by the mere rustling of a bag of sweets behind me in a Paris cinema. I whispered a slangy version of Shin's translation to Noiret, who had followed me and who sat writhing in merriment beside me.

After loudly applauding the victory of the revolutionary troops, I left the theatre with the silent blue-clad audience. I myself felt sadly proletarian, walking home in the rain dressed in my solitary suit, which was beginning to smell like a wet dog.

But that night my sadness quickly gave place to impatience for the next day to arrive. For we were going to see one of the great sights of the journey, one of the world's most fabulous monuments: the Great Wall of China.

# 7

It was a bright sunny day, with a cool breeze and sparkling light—normal weather, I was told, for October in Peking. Our coach left the capital through the old Tartar part of the city to the north-west. The clean, narrow streets were lined with old, grey, single storey houses with roofs of round grey tiles turned up at the edges. Outside the shops with their narrow wooden fronts were displays of baskets, apples, persimmons, nuts, vegetables, loaves of bread of various shapes, enamel ware and simple, attractive pots painted with flowers. Women were walking about with bulging shopping bags, and cyclists were gaily ringing their bells. Men and women were pulling wooden handcarts, carrying heavy baskets at the ends of long bamboo poles balanced across their shoulders, or pushing their children along in little bamboo carts. Soon the houses started thinning out, and before long the coach was driving up into hills turned to gold by the autumn foliage.

After an hour's drive we came out into the north-western plain, which was scattered with cornfields and planted with apple-trees and persimmon-trees. The road started winding again and at last we reached the Great Wall. What pictures those words conjure up for travellers sensitive to the romance of certain names! That day the Great Wall did not disappoint us. Within a ring of round, rocky, wooded mountains gilded by autumn and the sun, it appeared before us like a fabulous serpent stretching its coils across valleys, hills and mountains, occasionally raising a square tower towards the sky before plunging into a sheer mountain pass. A tiny ant in the face of this immensity, I said nothing, hypnotized by the grandiose beauty of the scene and horrified by the agony of the three hundred thousand prisoners of the Emperor Shih Huang-ti who built the wall. In the third century, thanks to the two thousand miles of this gigantic enterprise, Shih Huang-ti was able to repel the invading hordes of the Huns who fell back to hurl themselves instead on to Europe.

Staircases, walls and paved slopes followed one another. In the distance, in a powdery blue light, the first of the Manchu hills could be seen. I started to climb a tiny part of the Great Wall, while my companions scattered in different directions according to their inclinations and their mountaineering abilities.

The Chapeaus held hands and gazed at the landscape. Countess de Lissaye disappeared, to go and have a beer at the 'Great Wall Refreshment Room'. My little Swiss went off with a climbing party consisting of Isabella and her mother. The Blums got other members of the party to take photographs of them with their own camera. Noiret kept shooting me with his Leica, 'to have something in the foreground', and the Adjoufs just smiled admiringly.

Walking gently back to the village, overwhelmed by the beauty of the scenery and the transparent quality of the air, I stopped in front of an old woman and a young man, probably her son, who were sitting on the stone steps, eating little loaves of sesame. The old woman brought out a few grains of very white linseed. They both smiled at me. The young man said something to me, and a vague intuition led me to reply: *'Faguo* —France.' I saw from his vacant gaze that the word meant nothing to him. He went on speaking to me quietly. Unfortunately my intuition deserted me and all I could do was smile at him again.

I noticed that the old woman's feet had been bound in childhood: they were covered with tiny white cotton socks and encased in doll-size black felt slippers. When all the Chinese women of her age are dead, there will be no little feet left in China, for the appalling custom of binding girls' feet has been forbidden since the Revolution. She in her turn looked at my feet and roared with laughter at the sight of my nylon stockings and casual shoes.

We lunched in a restaurant at the foot of the Wall. In a room with bare walls a very good meal was served to us at little tables on immaculate cloths. In an adjoining room I noticed an English couple lunching with their interpreter: they seemed to be making heavy weather with their conversation. It was extremely cold and we were all wrapped up in several layers of sweaters. For once Pariet treated us to an excellent lecture on the geography of China, drawing from memory a superb map on a large sheet of white paper. Shin took notes of everything he said and translated the lecture in an undertone for Yuan, who seemed full of admiration. When Pariet had finished, the two of them went over to him and shook him warmly by the hand. Compared with my tourists from the other side of the world, they were much more eager to learn and seemed really happy when the opportunity was presented to them. Provided, of course, that the explanations were in accordance with the Party line. Much to my surprise, everybody had been extremely attentive. Only the Countess had nodded a little. Probably the beer.

On the way back, the trees looked even more golden and the light even softer. An hour's drive brought us to the tombs of the Mings. The plain, barred on the horizon by the grey and purple mountains we had just left, is crossed by a dead straight road lined on either side by a row of gigantic statues: dragons, elephants, tigers, hippopotami, horses, and guards in breastplates stand every ten yards along the ceremonial way leading to the great tomb of the Emperor buried inside a hill. At the entrance is a temple intended for anniversary ceremonies and the two kiosks built for the dignitaries who sealed the tomb and who were then executed to prevent them from divulging the place of burial.

The great vault is a huge room of splendid proportions, considerably restored. Inside are some admirable vases in white porcelain, decorated with flowers in which the oil for the lamp wicks used to be kept. The sight of these vases suddenly brought back a childhood memory to me. My parents had a similar, though less beautiful vase in their house. At every birthday party I had, one of my friends felt an irresistible urge to hide in it, and the vase was invariably shattered. After the party was over, I was given a spanking and the vase stuck together again until the following year.

In the museum adjoining the tomb, a small rectangular pavilion, the objects found in the tomb are displayed to the public: gold ingots, lumps of jade, bronze vases, and jewels belonging to the Empress and the concubine. I stopped to gaze in wonder at two vases of a special yellow hue—the funerary colour of the Emperors—and also at a perfect jade goblet. Marquis Torti seemed to share my admiration, and whispered in my ear that he had a large collection of Chinese *objets d'art* at Turin. Outside, the mountains were turning fawn, the sky pink and the leaves red. Two girls in white bonnets were weighing persimmons, which rolled about like big golden balls, in wooden baskets placed on a weighing-machine.

Back at the hotel, Shin joyfully announced a great piece of news to me: I had obtained an appointment with the Chinese doctor an English friend had suggested I should visit: Doctor Wong. Shin added with a shade of respect in his voice:

'He's a very important man: he's a member of the Consultative Assembly.'

I made a strange discovery when I got back to my room. The bottle of perfume I had left on my bedside table had disappeared. I found it a moment later carefully tucked away in my handbag. The hotel staff, I reflected, certainly took an interest in their guests...

Drinks and dinner with the Fayets. He was First Secretary at the French Embassy, a tall, good-looking man with a fiery gleam burning deep in his eyes. He had spent the whole of his childhood in China and spoke Chinese fluently. Every word he uttered revealed his love for this people among whom he had countless friends he could no longer see today because of the embarrassing situation he would put them in. They would in fact have to ask permission to come to see him and would subsequently have to provide a detailed report of everything which had taken place and been said during their visit. This would involve them in considerable inconvenience, with the added prospect of being placed on a list of suspected persons, which was not a prospect likely to appeal to anybody, however warm their feelings of friendship might be. Monsieur Fayet's fourteen-year-old son went to a Chinese school and spoke the language fluently like his father. He loved his school and had told his parents that he wouldn't leave it, even if his father was posted to another embassy. He had made some very good friends while at school, but outside school he was only allowed to meet them in the street.

We began discussing the Chinese passion for drawing up reports and putting everything into writing, a passion which originated in the Confucian cult of ancestors in which the biography of Great-Uncle No. 3 or of a fourth cousin twice removed was inscribed in detail on tablets exposed for the benefit of posterity in the hall of ancestors. On this subject our host told us the following story:

Two years before, the French cultural attaché had gone back to France on leave. He had an Alsatian he was very fond of, and as he could not take the dog with him he left it with the Fayets. One day Monsieur Fayet was summoned to the Foreign Ministry where an official gave him an extremely unpleasant reception and told him straight away that he would have to get rid of the animal. Surprised at being summoned to the Ministry for such a trivial reason, the diplomat replied that he could not comply with this request since the dog did not belong to him. He was curious, however, to learn the reasons for such a demand. The official then proceeded to read him a four-page report establishing the fact that the animal had knocked over a child two weeks earlier. But the report went even further back than that. Plunging into the mists of time, it revealed that three years before, not far from the Old Wall, the dog had pursued a soldier of the People's Army, forcing the man to hide in order to escape from the monster. On the 3rd of September the following year, in the village of Tien-Chi, it had likewise pursued the hens of an Agricultural Commune. Finally, a few months later, the brute had attacked an entire Chinese family. In these circumstances the representative of the French Government could not fail to understand how harmful such incidents were bound to be to Franco-Chinese relations...

# 8

The next morning I was due to meet Doctor Wong, and I was oddly excited at the prospect. Shu had ordered a taxi for me, or rather for the two of us. It was a new Shu who got into the car with me, a smiling, friendly Shu. She had taken her hands out of her pockets and she talked in a completely relaxed way. She told me that she was twenty-four, that she was engaged, and that she was going to be married in a few months. In order to limit the population explosion, apart from advocating birth-control, Chairman Mao, she told me, advised girls not to marry until they were twenty-five and boys to wait until they were thirty. And what about sexual relations outside marriage, I asked. Out of the question, she replied: they were absolutely forbidden. External and public displays of affection outside marriage were likewise prohibited, and were considered unseemly even between married couples—a case of traditional Chinese modesty reinforced by the austerity of the new régime.

Shu and her fiancé met every evening at their local club where they watched films or took part in political education meetings. There were dances too at the club, but Shu confided to me that she didn't like dancing. When I asked her whether it was his good looks which had drawn her to her fiancé, she replied like a child reciting a familiar lesson:

'Good looks are unimportant. I noticed my future husband because he obeys the rules laid down by Chairman Mao, because he knows Chairman Mao's writings by heart, and because he is a good citizen.'

Listening to Shu, I thought of my own daughter who was not quite fourteen and was mad about pop music and long-haired boys. Shu's mother obviously didn't have my problems!

I decided to press her harder.

'I can understand that, Shu, but all the same there's something else, isn't there?'

She made no reply, but watching her out of the corner of my eye, I saw a mysterious smile soften the lines of her impassive little face. Here again was the traditional modesty of the Chinese, a modesty of feeling as well as of word and deed. I pursued my inquiries no further.

We left Peking along some new avenues lined with trees planted since the Revolution and recently-built apartment houses. The taxi drew up in the courtyard of a modern three-storey building standing in the middle of a vast park: the Cancer Hospital built in 1958. I waited for a few minutes in an immaculate yellow-painted hall with a linoleum floor, while dozens of patients went by on their way to see a doctor. Naturally they did not look well, but they were all clean and all neatly dressed in the same navy-blue cotton tunics and trousers. A tall, bespectacled young man, dressed in grey trousers and a beige sweater over an open-necked white shirt, came to collect me. He looked like an American university student. He courteously led me along corridors painted a pale fawn colour to a small drawing-room furnished with a sofa, some deep leather armchairs, and a low table laid with tea bowls. From the wall Chairman Mao smiled benignly down at us. Following hard on my heels, Shu sat down in an armchair while I installed myself on the sofa. An orderly in a white smock served us the usual pale tea with some slightly nauseating green vegetation floating in it.

At this point Doctor Wong made a dramatic entrance. A rather portly figure, he was dressed in the surgeon's usual smock and skullcap, his cotton mask hanging under his chin. He had a florid complexion, smiled broadly, and exuded energy and gaiety. He shook hands with me warmly, apologized for having kept me waiting, explained that he had a great deal of work, and sat down beside me on the sofa. Speaking in French, he asked after Penelope, our English friend, and her five children. I replied in English, knowing that Shu would not understand. Following my example he started talking to me in English about his three children. When he got to the second, Shu muttered a few words to him in Chinese. He listened to her politely, and still speaking English, said to me:

'I'm afraid that your interpreter doesn't understand English.'

Somewhat taken aback, I asked whether that meant that we had to speak French. Ignoring my question, Doctor Wong smilingly continued the conversation, but this time in French. The gaiety of his attitude contrasted sharply with the seriousness in his eyes. I found him extremely likeable, with an unusually intense, radiant personality. He invited me to dinner at his house that very evening. Rather surprised, I replied that I was delighted by his invitation, but asked whether I shouldn't apply for permission to accept it. Slightly annoyed at this pusillanimous reaction, he exclaimed:

'Good heavens, no! Can you come about seven, because we go to bed early.'

I was overjoyed at the prospect. With this man, there could be no doubt that a dialogue would be both possible and interesting. And I was going to enjoy a unique experience for a tourist, in dining with a Chinese family. Perhaps Wong, accustomed to meeting European specialists on account of his Western background and medical career, was not submitted to the same surveillance and the same obligations as his fellow countrymen, and was thus able to enjoy greater freedom. I had reached this point in my astute deductions when I saw Shu get up and quietly leave the room.

The conversation began to drag a little. I had the feeling that the doctor's attitude had grown a little tense. I bravely went on talking at random, thinking that if I let the conversation languish there would no longer be any reason for me to stay and our meeting would have to come to an end.

Shu returned after a few minutes and spoke to the doctor in Chinese. He gave a curt little nod and turned towards me, frowning slightly.

'I'm terribly sorry about this evening,' he said. 'Your interpreter tells me that you have to go to the Opera. It seems that it's going to be very interesting.'

Silence fell between us. I felt suddenly upset as I looked at this learned man, with his open-minded outlook and rich sense of humour, who had to put up with such infuriating restrictions. No doubt because of his bourgeois origins he would forever remain a doubtful quantity in the eyes of a popular régime, which, however great his skill and devotion, would always suspect him of deviationism and bourgeois revisionism. A sort of mental claustrophobia overwhelmed me as I suddenly realized that *They* were right. A foreign education and a cosmopolitan upbringing do not predispose a man to unconditional intellectual submission, even if that man has freely offered his life and strength to the cause of the Revolution.

I sensed that Doctor Wong had guessed what I was thinking. He continued in a gentle voice:

'Don't upset yourself on my account. My life here is naturally very different from what it was in England, where I led the life of an English gentleman. I ran a clinic, had my tea at four o'clock, and finished work at five. But at the end of the war against Japan the public health situation here was so disastrous and the shortage of doctors so acute that I came back to place my skill at my country's service. Under the Chiang Kai-shek régime there was such corruption and waste that any individual effort was lost like a drop of water in the sea of misery that covered China. As you are probably beginning to see, an immense amount has been achieved since the Liberation. Obviously a great deal remains to be done. So you see, it is a great source of satisfaction, perhaps the greatest of all, to feel that one is being useful to one's people.'

Stirred by the passion in his words, I nodded approvingly. In the light of this ardent faith, the surveillance of an interpreter or any other kind of restriction could only seem unimportant to a man who had deliberately given up a pleasant, facile existence.

The doctor asked the man who was serving tea with the discreet efficiency of an English butler to go and fetch the duty photographer to immortalize our meeting. Then he stood up abruptly and offered to show me his office. I guessed that this proposal was intended to shake off Shu. In vain. My interpreter trotted behind us like a faithful dog and stationed herself in the doorway of a small room where the doctor sat down at a desk littered with files and papers. I settled down in the only armchair. Doctor Wong took two small rolls of paper out of a drawer, pictures by a modern artist which he handed to me, asking me to give one of them to the English friend who had suggested that I should call on him. Then, tipping himself back in his chair, he resumed the conversation in French. He asked me whether by any chance I had any medical acquaintances he might know. I thought straight away of a delightful man I sometimes see at Saint-Tropez, where he owns a house. He happens to be a communist. I mentioned his name on the off-chance that it might mean something to Doctor Wong. He gave a start.

'What!' he exclaimed. 'You know X!' And turning to Shu, he added: 'He is a very great French specialist!'

Shu's face lit up and I could feel her looking at me respectfully. A little embarrassed, I explained that I had met the man in question on a friend's yacht, and I mentioned a name famous in the communist world. Wong listened to me with a mischievous smile, and repeated:

'On So-and-so's yacht?'

I went on straight away to ask:

'Do you ever take a holiday?'

His face turned serious again.

'No, never,' he replied. 'There's too much work to be done and as yet there aren't enough doctors in China. We can't desert our patients.'

We went on talking like a couple of friends. I told him that I felt I was living through such an exceptional experience in China that international events would henceforth take on a new resonance for me. He then admitted how disturbed he was by the intense reactionary propaganda in Europe which depicted China as an aggressive, bellicose power.

'In fact,' he said, 'the only problem which preoccupies us today is the task of feeding, housing, clothing, caring for and educating seven hundred million people. A war would wipe out the gigantic efforts we are making. It would be an absolute disaster.'

He repeated the word *disaster* several times. I tried to reassure him.

'No,' I said, 'Europe isn't afraid of China. On the contrary, your country arouses immense interest in Europe, and countless books, articles and lectures are devoted to it. Only our extreme right-wing die-hards believe that China would want to start a third world war. Of course in the United States the situation is rather different.'

I had scarcely uttered these words before Doctor Wong stiffened. His features tightened. The topic was obviously a delicate one, at least in the presence of a third party. I quickly changed the subject and decided it was time to go. Shu's presence made it impossible to continue our conversation. We left the hospital together, followed by Shu. Taking leave of me, he told me how much he had enjoyed meeting me, and the 'breeze from the outside world' which our conversation had brought him. He shook hands warmly with me before I got into the taxi, expressed his regret at being unable to entertain me to dinner, begged me to call on him again if I returned to China, and waved to me until the taxi had driven out of the gate.

Somewhat shaken by this incursion into an existence which was so close to mine and yet so unfamiliar, I said unthinkingly to Shu:

'What an interesting man!'

'Yes,' was her only reply.

Did she have no opinion of her own? Or was this an attitude she had been ordered to adopt? Was Wong regarded as indispensable but untrustworthy?

On the way back to the hotel, I dropped in on Madame Fayet, who had kindly offered to lend me a few light clothes for the next stage of our journey in the south.

A bunch of delightful children, dressed in peony-coloured clothes, followed me, laughing, waving and shouting: 'Nikao—Hello!' Shu spoke to them, then explained to me that they were greeting 'a foreign friend of the Chinese people'. I swore under my breath. Did everything have to be explained, from the heat of the sun to the gaiety and friendliness of children? Still, I was becoming quite fond of Shu, even if she did sometimes get on my nerves. All of a sudden she asked me what I thought of the Chinese and listened attentively to my reply: I liked them very much, and thought they were intelligent, subtle, lively and courageous. I in my turn asked her whether in the course of her career as an interpreter she had noticed any differences between Western tourists according to nationality. She smiled.

'Oh, yes,' she said. 'The Italians are the most difficult of all. They grumble all the time and are hardly ever satisfied. The Germans are serious and very conscientious. The French are polite and very amusing.'

Although she was not a native of Shanghai, she made no comment on the English.

At the Summer Palace I rejoined my flock, who had visited a series of delightful monuments with ethereal names—the Temple of the Recumbent Buddha, the Temple of the Blue Cloud, and so on—which seemed to have left them an impression compounded of sunshine, pink walls, blue tiles, airy prospects, and exhilarating walks among mementoes of the formidable

Empress Tzu Hsi. For there, in that maze of countless gloomy, low-ceilinged little rooms, full of furniture, silks and *objets d'art*, there roams the ghost of the onetime courtesan who established a reign of terror and, among other charming habits, used to strangle her lovers once they had served their purpose.

A pretty walk along the shores of the silvery lake beside which she had a boat built of marble—with funds intended, needless to say, for the Chinese Navy—brought us to a pavilion where we ate a pleasant lunch washed down with cold beer. Odile Audiffret, the wife of one of the attachés at the Embassy, was with us. She was a tremendous success with everybody, for she knew the history of Peking in detail and recounted it with irresistible charm. My flock clustered round her, eating her up with their eyes. Marquis Torti and the Musketeers were lost in admiration, and even the women thought her 'a sweet little thing'.

Boarding some long wooden boats, with lattice-work stanchions painted red, and each handled by a single man who rowed in silence, we crossed the grey, silky lake in the golden afternoon light. The hills all around seemed to be melting into a mysterious mist, and there was nothing to be heard but the sound of the oars dipping into the water. Unfortunately this moment of graceful poetry was suddenly interrupted by a yell from Adrienne Mandois, accompanied by eloquent gesticulations:

'This outing is a dreadful bore! Let's go and do the antique shops!'

Immediately other complaints arose from all the boats, shattering the atmosphere as if it were crystal.

'I want to buy some mao-tai,' Signora Leandri announced in her Germanic accents.

'I'm cold,' howled the General.

I shut my eyes in exasperation, only to hear, echoed by the hills, an antiquarian litany:

'Antique shops ... antique ... antique ... ant ... ique.'

When I opened my eyes again, having recovered something of my composure, Odile whispered in my ear:

'Are they always like this?'

'Worse!' I replied.

Astonished by their visitors' capricious behaviour, the Chinese steered their boats towards the shore. Disembarkation was a perfect example of Latin pandemonium, with shouts, screams, thrusts, shoves, tumbles, and exclamations that differed from one person to the next. The Chinese rolled their eyes at this splendid demonstration of individualism, and Odile turned to me to say:

'I'm staying with you. I haven't seen anything like this for two years. Can I do anything to help?'

No, I told her; all I could do was wait for it to blow over. But when everybody had come ashore—without treating me to the pleasure of a single splash in the lake—they refused to get into the coach. Laure and Colette asked for a taxi to go to the Friendship Shop—the big local department store. The Musketeers said they would like to 'do the antique-dealers' by taxi. Signora Coli had an appointment with a woman friend at the Swedish Embassy. Adrienne Mandois had tummy-ache. Madame Blum insisted on going back to the Imperial City, again by taxi. Anybody would have thought we had all just come away from the showing of a collection at Dior's: everybody was shouting, gossiping, changing their mind, and hissing: 'Psst' to summon Shin ... or me. Finding half-a-dozen taxis at a moment's notice outside the Summer Palace was, I discovered, almost as difficult as arranging for a helicopter to land in the middle of the Place de la Concorde in Paris.

Between two howls from General de Boilèle I managed to get a word in to beg everybody to get into the coach, promising to drop off each and every one on the way. I got into the coach last of all, lit a cigarette, and stolidly refused to answer the subsequent bombardment of whens, hows and whys.

Our first stop was an antique shop. Boilèle rushed in ahead of everybody else, determined to get the best bargains for himself. Georges Wolf followed hard on his heels, equally determined to prevent him. By the time I arrived, bringing up the rear, the three small rooms of the shop looked like the Métro during the rush hour. In the showcases in the first room was a dusty collection of bull's-blood vases, willow-green bowls, and white porcelain decorated with flowers. These were all copies, of course, since antique dealers in China are not allowed to sell real antiques. In the next room, which was lined with showcases, Colette and Laure were picking out the best of hundreds of snuffboxes in every colour of the rainbow, for their private collection. Hands grasped eagerly at ivory sampans and pagodas, and statuettes in jade, cornelian, quartz and crystal. A fever of buying seemed to have taken hold of my tourists.

Madame Blum, whose son was an expert on Chinese antiques, was arguing with Noiret about the value of the cornelian statuettes. Madame Chapeau was clutching an ivory figure of a fisherman. In the heat of battle each person was clinging to his finds, terrified that his neighbour might find something better. Torti flew into a temper because Blum had bought a beautiful jade plaque he had marked out for himself. In one corner of the shop the Musketeers were buying dozens of knick-knacks to give as Christmas presents. Madame Neralinda, the plump little Peruvian banker's wife whose purchasing mania had never struck me till now, was amassing piles of odds and ends, buying anything and everything. The shop assistants looked pale and haggard, as the abacuses, infected by the general fever, clicked and clattered in an exotic cacophony. Five-yuan notes, the largest denomination in circulation, were brought out of wallets and purses in whole handfuls. The small round packets wrapped in pink paper looked like so many water-lilies. I literally had to rescue my pilgrims from their frenzy by force. It was an operation which took some time. I thought we were all back in the coach when little Neralinda came running along, almost hidden under dozens of water-lily parcels, and his wife's green eyes lit up with excitement. Everybody expressed astonishment at the low prices they had paid, and now at last, as we drove on, allowed themselves the luxury of admiring what their neighbours had bought.

Our next stop was the People's Market to the north-west of T'ien An Men Square. This turned out to be a huge covered market consisting of alley-ways lined with little shops which displayed quilted jackets and second-hand trousers hanging from rods, singlets (the only undergarment that exists in China), black felt slippers, rubber boots, glazed pottery and delightful floral porcelain, fur hats, and coats in rabbit fur, fox, sheep and mink (yes, mink, but a peculiar yellow colour!). I tried one on, and found myself looking at the reflection of Gloria Swanson in the dealer's mirror ...

Our little band of tourists scattered in all directions. Some of them disappeared into another antique shop full of treasures. The Italian women started clucking excitedly over a wig-dealer's stall, where for a few yuans, the brown-haired Madame Neralinda became the owner of a superb ebony wig. 'I'm going to have it dyed in Paris,' she said delightedly. I must admit that this heap of scalps sent a shiver down my spine and in spite of their spotless cleanliness made me feel slightly sick.

We roamed happily all over this flea-market without any fleas. Bicycles cost 120 yuans (about twenty pounds). Piles of old tyres were being cut into sandals by silent craftsmen. The stall-holders were all smiling, helpful and discreet, and only came up to us if we stopped. The alley-ways were quite crowded, with people strolling about and talking, the men looking, the women buying with coupons and stuffing their purchases into white string bags. There were stalls displaying apples, persimmons, vegetables, little pies, and all kinds of bread; there were also soup-kitchens where you could drink soup out of little porcelain bowls with spoons in matching porcelain. The sun turned red, the shadows purple, and darkness spread gently over the People's Market.

# 9

This morning we were due to travel by train to Loyang. At half-past five I went along the corridor knocking on each door in turn. The response I obtained revealed the occupant's true character in every case. At dawn self-control and the veneer of breeding are in abeyance, and there is nothing to mask grumpy, peevish or downright shrewish characters. The good-natured, on the other hand, are as good-natured as ever, and friends seem friendlier. Dupont, dear man, actually joked with me. Claire Adjouf greeted me as if she had only been waiting for me to make her day.

We left the hotel at half-past six. The citizens of Peking were actually doing physical jerks as they walked to their shops and offices. Cyclists in compact groups were silently making their way to work. Loudspeakers were playing snatches of Western military marches and Maoist propaganda speeches on every possible variation of the theme: 'Chairman Mao is our guide and saviour'. At the station, a modern building erected in 1950, with marble floors and pillars, a red carpet led to the platform between two rows of flowering shrubs. The train was waiting for us, sparkling in the sunlight. We were firmly guided towards our carriage which two men were busy washing and brushing. The entire carriage was reserved for us. Nobody would be allowed to pass through it except the ticket inspector, and the same would be true throughout our stay in China. Each compartment contained four bunks which were already made up, with delightful flowered satin eiderdowns and white sheets buttoned down on the underside. A table between the two lower bunks carried an ashtray and four white porcelain teapots decorated with blue flowers.

Although the strictest honesty was obviously observed everywhere, with people running after you with the laddered stocking you had thrown away or the empty pillbox you had left on the dining-room table—I even recovered in this way the Sheraton matches I had left behind at the famous conference with Yuan—Boilèle started shouting that we should make sure our luggage was on the train. Everybody began running up and down the corridor yelping in alarm before the bewildered eyes of our mentors. I intervened curtly to restore calm. The luggage was of course all in its proper place at the end of the carriage, and soon everyone had plunged under their eiderdown to sleep or read. This was another little proof of the special treatment the Chinese give their foreign tourists; their compartments are made up for sleeping all day. A few minutes later an attendant dressed in blue and equipped with hardly any teeth came along and put a spoonful of green tea in each teapot, after which another attendant, who unlike the first was very well provided with teeth, filled the teapots with hot water from a copper watering-can with a long spout.

A few moments later a woman in blue appeared with her hair done up in a white scarf and started frantically sweeping the floor, sending into our nostrils clouds of coal dust (all Chinese trains run on coal), which had been lying quite happily where it was. This procession of attendants continued at the same rate all day long. At seven o'clock in the morning, loudspeakers installed in every compartment started instructing us in the thoughts of Chairman Mao. As we were unable to benefit greatly from this facility and we were the only people in the carriage, Shin agreed to switch off the loudspeakers. The day went by in a gentle routine of social calls, conversations, reading and dozing. The scenery was very strange: high hills of sepia-coloured loess, the providential alluvial soil of China, cut into squares and separated by straight corridors. Not a single tree, not a single road, and hardly any houses. Here and there a village of dried mud huts with thatched roofs, or, in the case of the larger houses, roofs of round tiles. Here there were no turned-up ridge tiles: the region was too poor. There were some cultivated fields on the hillsides, but they were few and far between. On the paths an occasional cart could be seen, being pulled by a donkey, a man, or a woman. A few pigs and hens were rooting about or pecking at the ground, but there were no sheep or cattle, for pasture-land is a luxury the Chinese cannot afford. Nor could I see any dogs—but dogs are a delicate subject in China, for Westerners maintain that they were all eaten by the Chinese during the great famines of 1946 when millions of people starved to death: when you speak of the disappearance of the dogs, the Chinese wax indignant, or change the subject.

The temperature started rising and the light grew harsher. I switched on the ventilator in my compartment, which stopped after ten minutes and only started up again an hour later, for another ten minutes, just like my little bedside lamp.

About eleven o'clock the train stopped at Anyang, a little town which already existed in the Bronze Age and which has recently become a thriving industrial centre. We all got out, to find ourselves in a red-painted station decorated with coloured murals and crowded with market stalls selling cakes, loaves of bread, superb apples and other fruit, and paper flowers. Each stall was surrounded by swarms of travellers who stared at us inquisitively. There were a lot of young men in dungarees and soft caps; a few families, the youngest children firmly strapped to the backs of their mothers or elder sisters; and soldiers in plain, indistinguishable uniforms, all external signs of rank having been abolished in 1965. The soldiers we met here and everywhere else in China behaved with the same calm courtesy as the rest of the population. The luggage of the other travellers consisted of pretty, fragile wickerwork cases or bundles hanging from the end of a pole carried over the shoulder. Now and then a plastic suitcase could be seen, carried by a gabardine-clad Party official. During our stop at Anyang, railway workers gave our train an energetic wash-and-brush-up.

Isabella, the pretty young Italian girl in our group, was busy trying the effect of her charms on Shin. The Mandois's wig was sparkling in the sunshine. The Musketeers filled my arms with apples, paper flowers and little cakes, at the same time ogling the Chinese girls and giving vent to schoolboyish expressions of admiration such as: 'Look at that one! What a smasher!' You had to have a sharp eye or be very sex-starved to find any beauty in those women with their badly cut hair, shapeless trousers and neglected complexions. Heavy work has turned the dainty little Chinese girls of our Western imaginations into sexless creatures who stride along like Grenadier Guards, but with their hands in their pockets. These girls were short and stocky, but gay and sweet-natured. None of them returned the Musketeers' lewd glances.

73

The train moved off again. For the first time, on that station platform, we had had the impression of being at the very heart of China. About one o'clock in the afternoon we stopped at another station. Shin made us get out and took us along to the restaurant car where we were served a good Chinese meal on flower-decked tables, to the accompaniment of apologies for the unworthiness of the dishes we were being offered. It was very hot, the windows wouldn't open, and we lunched quickly in a sticky atmosphere. I asked for permission to go back to our carriage, only to be told that we would have to wait until the next stop at half-past three. I tackled Yuan with a long homily in the Chinese manner, full of compliments and apologies, explaining that we were unaccustomed to the climate, that we were suffering from the heat, and that if need be I was quite capable of pulling the alarm signal to stop the train. For the first time I had the feeling that the smile Yuan gave me was not confined to his teeth. He launched into a flood of apologies about the climate, our sufferings, the unworthiness and discomfort of the meal, and all that remained to be done in that and other respects, adding that he would do his best to meet all our criticisms, and that of course he gave us permission to go down the train to our compartments. Descending from our olympian heights, we prepared ourselves for a brief contact with suffering humanity. Chinese railways, we discovered, appeared to have two classes. In the first-class carriages there were four bunks to each compartment, without mattresses or eiderdowns, and separated from the corridor by a curtain. Whole families were crowded together in these compartments, the men in singlets, the women nursing their babies. In the corridor, above a narrow shelf running along the carriage which held enamel tea-bowls, hung the passengers' face-cloths.

The second-class passengers sat in pairs, face to face, on wooden benches separated by tables placed under the windows. On these tables stood the traditional enamel tea-bowls. The general impression was one of overcrowding and poverty, but everything was clean and there were no smells. Cleanliness is in fact one of Mao's commandments, and is regarded as a national duty. Pariet told us that the absence of any physical odour among the Chinese was due to the shortage of fish and meat in their diet.

We were now crossing the fertile Hopei plain, which was

covered with cornfields and nurseries protected from the wind by stone walls built in semi-circles. The fields bristled with memorial stones—vestiges of the past which the Government had tried to remove in order to increase the arable area, only to meet with such opposition that it had been forced to abandon the attempt. I caught sight of a group of six peasants pulling a wooden plough while a seventh man kept the ploughshare moving in a straight line.

The afternoon dragged on, hot and sticky. To relieve our boredom, Pariet gathered us together in three compartments and gave us a little lecture on North-Western China, the Chansi and Shensi provinces towards which we were travelling. Most of us learned for the first time that Shensi, the final point of the Long March, had always been the great bastion of Chinese communism. In the very first months of its existence, the People's Government had accordingly set out to irrigate, equip and industrialize that undercultivated and underpopulated region. To begin with, they had had to extend the railway from Peking to the province of Sinkiang, which was rich in minerals, and transfer to that province whole populations who were starving in the overpopulated ricefields of the South-Eastern coastal areas or crowded together in the slums of Shanghai and Canton. This draconian policy had been aimed at establishing a better distribution of the population and suppressing the underdeveloped areas. At this point my pilgrims started sniggering. Why? In the name of the sacrosanct principles of freedom? What freedom? The freedom to starve to death? It seemed to me that of all freedoms that was the one it should be easiest to sacrifice.

Noiret, my mini-Caesar, asked what was the attitude of Mao's Government towards birth control, and Pariet launched out into another little lecture in three stages. During the 'hundred flowers' period, in other words in 1956, when Mao had tried to introduce freedom of speech, freedom of thought and freedom of the press, and to encourage criticism provided it was constructive, a huge campaign had been launched to promote birth control. Though backed up by lectures given by doctors and nurses in both town and country, it had been an almost total failure. The illiterate masses had remained hostile and impervious to the Government's propaganda and the idea of this radical change in age-old customs. To avoid losing face completely, the Government had given up the attempt, announcing *urbi et orbi* that China needed all its children to repopulate its Western provinces and that man was the only effective weapon against the nuclear weapons of the Imperialists. This had brought to an end the 'hundred flowers' period which had produced a tidal wave of criticism whose vitriolic violence had endangered the very existence of the régime. Mao had abruptly altered course, and China had become a huge, seething cauldron of autocriticism, trials for 'revisionism', arrests, disappearances and 're-education' in distant communes.

Since the meeting between Krushchev and Eisenhower at Camp David in 1957, China had worked out a new political philosophy: as Russian collusion with American Imperialism left China isolated, she could survive only by the overwhelming number of her inhabitants. Or as Mao had declared: 'Even if the United States kill four hundred million Chinese with their atom bombs, three hundred million will be left to rebuild the country.' The fact remained that while they were waiting for the atom bombs to be dropped, China had to feed seven hundred million inhabitants, three hundred and sixty-five days a year. That was why, as Shu had explained to me, the régime 'recommended' the Chinese not to marry before twenty-five in the case of women and thirty in the case of men. Abortion was allowed for families which already had three children. Mao himself advised the Chinese not to have more than two children and the parents of large families to have themselves sterilized.

Listening to these explanations, the Italian women in the group uttered little cries of disgust while the Frenchwomen remained silent. As for the men, they all pulled horrified faces, confusing fecundity and virility in a common Mediterranean reaction.

Outside, the number of cultivated fields was growing smaller. The earth was brown and bare, with cracks across it here and there. Walls, curved like giant shin-bones, protected trees which themselves looked like skeletons in the brief dusk.

# 10

About half-past ten at night we arrived at Loyang, after travelling for fourteen and a half hours to cover just over four hundred miles. It had been a slow but on the whole pleasant journey, full of the sweet charm of an enclosed, rather *fin de siècle* world in which life went on against a slowly changing background. An irreproachable welcome awaited us. On the platform Shin introduced us to three men in gabardine coats who led us courteously to a coach where we were given the numbers of our rooms. The foyer of the hotel, on the other hand, was rather shabby, with a cement floor and peeling white walls; but the rooms were quite pleasant and the staff smiling. At dawn the next day, opening one eye and jumping into a rough stone bathtub, I thought to myself how lucky I was to be able to see Loyang. Hardly any foreigners have been allowed to visit this little old town which used to sleep peacefully inside its walls and which Mao has turned into one of the biggest industrial centres in the country. In less than fifteen years the population of Loyang has risen from fifty thousand to six hundred thousand inhabitants. I felt a joyful curiosity about this little town which had become a huge city. At last I had reached the heart of the unknown China where there were no white men, the inaccessible, closely guarded, mysterious China I had dreamt about since childhood. Wriggling my toes in the rust-coloured bathwater, I let a wave of happiness roll over me. I knew deep down that nothing could dispel my satisfaction at having fulfilled this old ambition. I was already bewitched by China and the affection I felt for this country could only grow deeper.

Coming back to earth, I thought about the programme I had worked out with Yuan the night before on a wooden chair under the blinking electric light bulb which hung from the ceiling of the bleak hotel foyer. I went down to the dining-room for breakfast and found Laure chatting with a wrinkled waiter who informed us in French that he was fifty years old. It was amusing to hear an inhabitant of Loyang who was neither a teacher nor an interpreter speaking a very lively, almost slangy French. He had been a steward for several years on a French steamer and was obviously delighted to be able to joke with us and tell us his life story, for he burst out laughing after every sentence. But when two other waiters arrived he corrected the situation, giving a slight bow and walking away with a smile. Soon my little party had gathered together in the dining-room for a pleasant breakfast. Only Colette and Madame Chapeau were missing. I found them still in bed, flu-ridden, feverish, pale and catarrhal, and comforted them as best I could with aspirins and kind words.

Our destination that day was Lungmen, one of the great sanctuaries of Chinese art, which had been closed to foreigners since the Revolution. On our way there our coach drove through the modern Loyang of half a million new inhabitants, a modern city with broad tree-lined avenues, three-storeyed concrete houses, parks full of flowers and big shopping centres. There were a great many cyclists on the road, for it was nearly time for work to begin in the offices and shops. Then we found ourselves out in the country, golden and beautiful in the morning sunshine. Maizefields were followed by cornfields, dotted with colourful pyramids of ripe melons. A few peasants were already at work, generally in groups of six. The road was crowded with hundreds of carts drawn by donkeys, men or women. Sometimes these carts contained several children, sometimes a solitary old man jolting up and down with every rut and every hole in the road. But more often than not they were laden with big oval baskets full of rags, coaldust or maize. Shu proudly pointed out to me that the wheels of these humble vehicles were nearly always equipped with rubber tyres, 'which produce a reduction in friction and noise'.

I was constantly being reminded how concerned the Chinese are about the problems of noise and dirt, and how stubbornly they are trying to deal with them. The accounts of travellers who knew the China of old are full of mentions of shouting and excrement, of the stench of the towns and the filthiness of the villages. Present-day China on the other hand seems to be in

78

habited by people who talk in measured tones, except of course for the announcers whose voices, generously amplified by loud-speakers, scatter to the four winds praise of Chairman Mao and exhortations to all the civic virtues, notably silence. As nearly all the arable land in China is tilled by manual labour, and all farm produce transported in carts, there can be no doubt that the use of tyres has reduced the noise of vehicles in both town and country. Another remarkable improvement which the visitor can observe is the elimination of the fly. That minor scourge of ancient China has now been virtually abolished. I was to meet only one fly in the whole of my journey—in Nanking—and then I politely pretended not to have seen it. During the first few years of the new régime it was the civic duty of every good Chinese to kill at least six flies a day!

After an hour's drive, the coach crossed the Loyang River, a lazy yellow river which winds its way across gentle hilly country. On its banks I caught sight of my first tractor. Shin swore to me that it was Chinese. In the midst of that vast expanse it looked tiny and somewhat pathetic, a real treasure which saved dozens of men the backbreaking work of carrying crush-ing burdens on their calloused shoulders.

As we drew near our destination I felt quite feverish with excitement. Lungmen is Buddha's China. On the walls of the grottoes carved out of the rocks—there are over three thousand of them—is a fantastic gallery of sculptures which the art experts of the West describe as one of the marvels of Chinese art. Looking upwards, I found myself face to face with a serenely ironic Buddha flanked by his grimacing guardians and groups of miniature Buddhas cut out of the grey-gold cliff. The huge cliff covered with rank weeds and wild flowers serves as a roof and shelter for this fantastic creation of the Weis, dating back to the fifth and sixth centuries A.D. Getting our breath back after this Rabelaisian appetizer, we followed Pariet along the right bank of the river. He took us into the first grottoes, where we could just make out in the shadowy background the tradi-tional group of Buddha and his guardians. These, the oldest of the Lungmen sculptures, date back to the famous Han period, from the second century B.C. to the second century A.D., which was to Chinese art what Greco-Roman art was to our civilization. The carving is stiff and massive but vigorous, and the faces are impressive in spite of a certain fixity. My pilgrims were trans-

fixed with admiration, especially Torti who gave ecstatic clucking noises. Only Pariet seemed unaffected, and muttered a few
grumpy commonplaces. In the third grotto I dug him in the
ribs.

'For God's sake,' I said, 'let's have a bit of lyricism! Say anything that comes into your head—give us a description, a commentary, a few anecdotes.'

Scowling more than ever, he retorted disdainfully:

'I can't help it. I haven't got an artistic mind.'

Heaven help me! Here I was, stuck in Loyang, at the far end
of the world, in the very depths of China, with a dear little man
who 'hadn't got an artistic mind'. I stifled a groan and we
went on with our tour. Behind me I heard Boilèle complaining,
for once with some justification:

'That idiot doesn't know a thing! It's a swindle!'

The others too, even the friendly ones, started grumbling.

'He's rather dry, your little pal,' Noiret hissed at me. I sympathized. I had been in a rage ever since the first grotto. I could
have strangled Pariet ... and myself as well for good measure ...
Though I went on fuming, I couldn't help being charmed by
the smiling spirituality of the Wei Buddhas, the first to acquire
a few draperies. In the Grotto of the Thousand Buddhas I got a
little of my breath back and tried to remedy to the best of
my limited ability the deficiencies of our 'cultural adviser'.
This grotto, which is completely lined with statuettes of smiling
Buddhas carved out of the rock, is a miracle of delicate harmony.
The T'ang period which the following grottoes revealed to us
drew fresh cries of admiration. Much to my relief, everybody
forgot Pariet and gazed in fascination at the flowing draperies
and fuller faces which foreshadowed Indo-Aryan art. I chattered
on, rather shamefacedly, and apart from Torti everybody listened to me kindly. The last accessible grotto turned out to be
partly hidden under the cliff and partly fallen in. Coming out, it
was pleasant to feel the gentle caress of the sun on my face and I
took a deep breath of the spicy air. The river glistened like
brown satin under the midday sun. I filled my eyes with the
gold-tinted landscape with the elegant arch of the modern
bridge silhouetted against it. Our party split up. We had half
an hour before lunch, so I went back for a last visit to my
favourite grottoes. In one I found Georges and the little Swiss,
in another Laure, and then nobody. Walking slowly back to-

wards the restaurant, and lingering on a delicate little arched bridge made of carved white stone, I noticed Adrienne Mandois sitting in the back of the coach. Heavens, I thought, she must be ill again! And I rushed over to the coach to find out what was wrong.

'Why, no, my dear,' she murmured, 'I'm perfectly all right. But what do you expect me to do in your grottoes? In any case, I'd have forgotten everything in ten minutes!'

I looked at her in horror, dumbfounded by this offence against the human spirit, and choking with indignation and contempt. I found myself positively snarling at the thought of certain friends of mine who would have given a great deal to be there, and not to sit in the back of a coach either, nor to pontificate about China at society dinner-tables during the following season.

The great Buddha looked utterly placid, indifferent to the torments of the soul. I sat down at the entrance to one of the grottoes and once again felt appeased by the cool serenity and unchanging peace of the place.

Another surprise was waiting for me. On the terrace of the restaurant my so-called art-lovers had already forgotten the few precious hours they were living through in this unique spot to which they would never return. They were laughing and drinking beer.

Dear, wonderful Chinese beer! I offered up thanks for it after seeing the effect it had on little Pariet. At last he started talking, giving a few dates, telling an occasional anecdote. He hadn't turned into a second Demosthenes of course, but at least my stomach cramps disappeared. My companions too were more relaxed. The river turned pink and it seemed to me that everyone was steeped in the idyllic calm of the scene, even Yuan, whom I asked for permission for us to go for a walk in old Loyang on our way back. He agreed at once, as he did almost every time I asked him for some favour.

On the way to Loyang the coach stopped outside the majestic wooden temple of Kuanling which had been turned into a museum of Neolithic tools and pottery. The display was well presented and the exhibits were in very good condition. While our party was inspecting the collection with every sign of interest, a voice suddenly reached us from the bottom of the garden. It was Boilèle shouting:

81

'We're wasting our time here! No, I refuse to budge an inch to go and see a lot of old pots!'

Pariet, who was at last beginning to show a little animation, was hurt and disgusted, and retired into a stubborn silence from which he emerged only for a few exchanges with the Chinese. Luckily our next stop, the temple of Kuankong, brought a smile back to the old General's lips. A real smile too! Torti also went into ecstasies over the enormous collection of T'ang pottery, the dozens of statuettes of dancers, favourites, cameleers with or without camels, and horses with or without riders, all protected by glass panes dark with dust and insect droppings (though not, I need scarcely say, fly droppings). Every one of these pieces would be worth a fortune in the West. Boilèle, as it happened, possessed a few specimens of this period in his private collection, and his delight brought him to the verge of tears. This emotion made him almost likeable for a moment; but just as my heart was beginning to soften towards him, I heard him thundering at Shin:

'It's an absolute scandal displaying treasures like these so badly! In a European museum, every one of these wonderful pieces would be exhibited in a separate showcase and not left in this dusty pile.'

I felt a shiver run down my spine as Shin translated this masterpiece of diplomacy for Yuan's benefit. Yuan said nothing, but his smile vanished as if it had been wiped off his face. Shin looked embarrassed. Laure, dear, subtle Laure, saved the situation by cooing maliciously:

'The European museums couldn't leave their rare Chinese pieces in a pile even if they wanted to, because they haven't got enough to make a pile of.'

This was a clever remark to make, since the Chinese consider that the works of art from their country which are in foreign museums have been stolen from them.

There was intense activity in the fields, where wooden ploughs were being drawn by teams consisting of a horse and a donkey, an ox and a horse, or a donkey and an ox. There were not enough draught-animals, Shin explained, to have the same animals in each team. The countryside was full of little groups of bent-backed peasants. Every now and then they would straighten up and, resting on their scythes, chat happily together. We stopped for a moment beside a cottonfield, a vast brown expanse studded with white flowers being picked by women and children. We took photographs of a mother and son, a boy about ten years old, who were gazing at us inquisitively. Signora Negri remarked in her shrill, sour voice:

'Shin, I thought that child labour had been abolished and that all Chinese children went to school.'

'That is correct,' Shin replied imperturbably, 'but nobody can prevent a child from helping its mother after it comes home from school.'

A little farther on, I noticed a couple of ancient tractors in a cornfield. China imported and manufactured tractors, Pariet explained, in order to free labour in agricultural areas to be sent to regions which were still undeveloped.

'But we are still very short of motorized transport,' Shin broke in, thus anticipating the sneers and sniggers of the Boilèle-Mandois group.

On the road, we overtook long lines of carts pulled by tired, bent, hollow-faced men. As soon as we stopped in the old part of Loyang, a crowd gathered round us and followed us through the narrow streets. They didn't make fun of us, and wanted nothing more than to smile at us. In the eyes of these men and women living in the depths of China we could only be friends of the Chinese people since we were there in their country. Somebody in our group clapped his hands and soon we were surrounded by a loud circle of applause which went on until we got back into the coach. Three girls asked me where I came from.

'*Faguo,*' I replied; 'France.'

They looked at me uncomprehendingly. It was obvious that the name of that part of their planet meant nothing to them.

'They are only country girls,' said Shin to excuse them.

Suddenly they burst out laughing, pointing to my shoes and stockings. Feeling like a reigning monarch, I slowly walked along the narrow streets lined with little houses of brick and sometimes mud, with grey tile roofs. Through the open doors I caught sight of long narrow yards in which men in singlets and women in light smocks were sitting round rickety old tables, chatting and drinking tea. Squatting in front of one door, a couple of old men were playing cards on the beaten earth. Some old women with bound feet, wearing the traditional long black tunic, with their hair done in tight little chignons, were holding small children by the hand. The role of the grandmother in modern China is very important, for in most families both father and mother go out to work and it is the grandmother who looks after the children. There are still not enough schools and kindergartens, especially in recently developed areas, to cope with a rising birthrate.

One street stall followed another: mainly displays of vegetables, fruit or rice. A cooper was hammering lustily at a metal bar. His neighbour the coppersmith was working in the narrow corridor of his house. Farther on, as in Peking, a cobbler was cutting sandals out of old tyres. Both yards and streets were very clean, sometimes even scrubbed spotless. What I could see of the insides of the houses struck me as poor and bare but polished and tidy. The children were round, pink, healthy and well-fed. The clothes people were wearing were often patched with pieces of material in different colours, but they were all clean. Nobody was dressed in rags, except for a very old man with a long white beard who ambled along in tatters, looking pitifully haggard. As we turned a corner into a narrow alley-way, an ecstatic Pariet dragged me into a bookshop, a big dark room lined with shelves sagging under the weight of thousands of volumes. A portrait of Mao indicated which way the wind—the East wind—blew. Pariet was looking for a geography book. A charming salesgirl with a pigtail smilingly informed him that she was not allowed to sell him any of the books in the shop. Pariet smiled back and retorted in Chinese:

'Why not? Do you take me for a spy? Even if I *were* a spy, don't you think that with their satellites the Americans have already photographed everything that interests them about the geography of China?'

The girl burst out laughing, and, completely convinced, brought him three dusty volumes which he accepted reverentially, promising, as she had requested, that 'nobody would know anything about it'.

The little square in which the coach was waiting for us was packed with people. Noiret started the clapping game again. The crowd followed his lead, clapping frantically and smiling. Suddenly Pariet caught fire and, with an eloquence I had unfortunately never encountered in him before, spoke to the crowd in Chinese. Going wild with joy, the onlookers enthusiastically applauded every sentence he uttered, almost splitting

84

their sides with laughter. They were nearly all very young and it was amusing to find oneself in the midst of a sea of laughing eyes and flashing smiles. Watching Pariet as he went on talking, I indulged in some solemn reflections on the magic of language. What wonderful vehicles for thought and feeling words were, and what powerful bulldozers with which to break through frontiers and into hearts! If we all spoke the same language, everybody would inevitably end up by being moved by something his opponent said. Everything would be possible.

The rearguard of our party gradually caught up with us, likewise surrounded by its milling escort. Adrienne Mandois was simpering, smiling, waving her gloved hand, uncertain whether to imitate Chairman Mao or the Queen of England. For my part, this was the first time since I had arrived in China that I had had the impression of living in a human ant heap.

# 11

Splitting up into two groups, my pilgrims went off in the radiant, scented morning air towards two very different destinations. The first group, led by Pariet, was going to visit a ball-bearings factory, the second biggest factory of its kind in China. As for me, I was taking my chattering little party to school.

Walking in single file, we crossed a pretty little courtyard planted with flowers and trees, where we were greeted by a young headmistress with a warm smile and an intelligent face. Shu acted as our interpreter. In a white-walled room which opened on to the garden, we sat down for the traditional preliminary conference round a table on which we were served the usual pale tea with big green leaves floating in it, under Chairman Mao's fatherly gaze. This headmistress, all buttoned up in her black suit, with her basin crop and her finely chiselled features, seemed very likeable. She spoke in a low voice. It was terribly frustrating, not understanding what she was saying, thus losing all the shades of meaning which Shu's monolithic mind obviously failed to appreciate and which in any case, translated into her inadequate French, reached us only in the form of basic facts and figures. We were in Tsing-Tse school which had 1,330 pupils, 95% of whom were the children of workers and peasants, and 52 teachers and employees. It covered an area of 1,000 square yards compared with 550 square yards in 1947, when it had had only 270 pupils, nearly all of them from landowning families and the upper middle class. In passing we were courteously asked to remember that Chairman Mao had stated that 'education must be used for the benefit of the people and combined with manual labour to rid the minds of the intellectuals of any idea of class superiority'.

In 1958, we were told, the school had set up some small workshops where the children could go after school and follow whatever pursuits they chose. We were going to visit those work-shops. The ladies in my party were all very attentive, except for Adrienne Mandois who gave a huge yawn which showed us every one of her crown fillings.

Since the Liberation, the headmistress doggedly continued, 3,311 pupils had left the school with a primary school leaving certificate. The best of them had gone on to secondary school, while the rest had gone to work in the fields and factories where some of them had become 'star workers'.

All this inevitably struck us as rather naïve and boring, yet the fact remained that this campaign against illiteracy conducted by zealous and devoted men and women like our headmistress was overcoming the superstition and ignorance of an uneduca-ted, backward peasantry.

Instead of such Utopian abstractions we were treated to the edifying story of Comrade Hu-Sin-Shua, who was not only a very lazy pupil but full of evil instincts. For example she hated manual labour, while on the other hand she had a lively penchant for private ownership. Well, now she was one of the star workers in the town; she had become an excellent waitress.

'Pooh! A waitress!' sneered the vamp. 'That's nothing to boast about.'

I was bound to admit that to our enlightened Western minds these naïveties were rather irritating. But, soft-hearted creature that I am, I was deeply touched by this headmistress for whom life had a meaning because she had helped to rescue three thous-and children from the hopeless quagmire of ignorance. Dupont's Genevese accent brought a smile back to my lips as he broke in with assumed bonhomie:

'Oh, being a waitress isn't so bad. Twenty years ago her starving parents would probably have sold her to the first comer at the roadside.'

That was enough talking: the tour of the school was due to begin. First the music room, where a graceful young woman with long plaits and gentle features sat at a little old piano playing with her slender fingers a tune which sounded like a harpsichord melody. She sang a song in a sweet voice and a score of little dolls with pink cheeks and red smocks repeated the refrain, at the same time imitating the flight of a butterfly.

Next it was the turn of the radio workshop, a large room in

which about thirty ten-year-olds were sitting around a long table. Each child was working with intense concentration on his own little transistor radio, performing delicate welding operations by dipping tiny tools into a pot containing a little molten metal. Unlike France, where visitors to a school are usually greeted with noisy, giggling curiosity, here you could have heard a pin drop, the silence was so complete.

In the paintshop the boys were sandpapering little wooden boxes which the girls painted red and then covered with a coat of varnish. These boxes were destined to house the transistor radios being assembled in the next room. Again there was complete silence, not a single eyelid was raised, not a single gaze followed us around. I felt almost intimidated.

The same concentration was to be seen in the scale-model workshop. But here, to my astonishment, a little girl with a skin as downy as an apricot was having trouble with the wings of her model aircraft which insisted on slipping to one side. She heaved a noisy sigh of exasperation and her little face took on the same expression, half-sad, half-angry, that I had often seen on my daughter's face when she was having trouble with a difficult Latin translation. This explosion of anger in the midst of all those little well-trained robots filled me first of all with amused relief, then with a certain anxiety. That little girl was going to have trouble. Her explosive individualism would have to be subjugated and 'brought into line'. Devotion to the collective good and disciplined efforts in that direction were incompatible with impatience and independence. I sadly foresaw many difficult days and many nights of autocriticism for my unknown little friend.

The most astonishing part of the whole school was the Morse code class. A young teacher was dictating a text to his pupils, and the whole room resounded with the clicking of transmitters. Every Chinese child, the headmistress explained, had to be able to take part in the defence of his country in the event of an attack. As a result, at the first warning, a huge intelligence network would promptly cover the whole of China.

Next we came to the kindergarten. All my dear ladies gave vent to cries of delight and surprise at the door of each of the white-painted rooms furnished with little beds and low tables in light-coloured wood. The chubby, red-cheeked infants, their eyes flashing like sparks of fire, sang for us in piping voices what my companions called 'charming, adorable songs'. These chants were in fact hymns in praise of Uncle Mao and called down destruction upon the capitalist invaders.

The Mandois woman, in an admirable show of motherly affection, swooped down on a tiny little boy, grasped him in an octopus-like gesture, and pressed him frantically to her bosom. Although courtesy and self-control are national virtues practised all over China, I don't think I have ever heard such fantastically loud howls come from such a small body as came from that little Chinese. Shin, Isabella and I nearly split our sides laughing. The terror of the poor infant as he saw that huge scarlet mouth approaching his little cheeks and felt himself being crushed in the arms of that white-skinned she-devil must have been all the more overwhelming in that people don't kiss in China. Never in public, certainly; possibly in private; but in any case not at the drop of a hat as in France.

The headmistress looked at us and smiled her beautiful smile. She was surrounded by a sort of radiance, and gave off a definite charm. You felt that she was tranquil and fulfilled. Isabella and I returned her smile with a certain respect. Chatting with us all the time, she led us back to the conference room, where she told us we could ask her any questions we liked about the school.

Pierre Adjouf started the ball rolling.

'What proportion of the national budget is devoted to education?' he asked.

The headmistress replied that 'the Government gives what is necessary'.

'Is education compulsory?' asked Doctor Blum. 'And if so, are there sufficient schools?'

The young woman replied that since the Liberation the number of schools had grown rapidly. Now over ninety-five per cent of the country's children went to school.

One of the Italian women in our group wanted to know how many years a child spent at school before going to University.

'From seven to fourteen, children go to primary school,' replied the headmistress, 'then to secondary school until the age of twenty. After that they have a chance of entering University.'

'Let's go,' cried Adrienne Mandois. 'I'm bored stiff.'

Back at the hotel, I went straight away to see how Colette Quesnel was feeling. I found her feverish and depressed, and felt worried about her condition. Accompanied by Shu, I appealed to the hotel manager, a calm, courteous man with a slim figure (the traditional 'fat Chinaman' was obviously a thing of the past). He telephoned straight away for a doctor and had tea served for us while he went back to his papers. The doctor arrived five minutes later, a man of about forty with steel-rimmed spectacles and a fawn gabardine suit. Like the hotel manager, he spoke only Chinese. This meant that he had done all his training in China, since most doctors aged over forty had studied in the United States or Europe. I took him to see his patient. Expecting to be examined, she pushed away the sheet and blanket which she had pulled right up to her nose. To our surprise, the doctor stopped her with a gesture, stood in the doorway of the room, put his hand to his own throat and coughed, at the same time raising his eyebrows in mute inquiry. Colette nodded, brandishing the thermometer with one hand while with the other she indicated that she had a very high temperature. The strange long-distance examination was already over. The doctor, still as far away as ever, wrote out a very pretty prescription in Chinese characters and handed it to Shu. Then he bowed in the direction of his patient without so much as looking at her, and disappeared, leaving us in a state of some perplexity. Shu seemed surprised at our bewilderment. She explained that no Chinese doctor would ever take the liberty of examining a woman. This was the explanation of those charming ivory statuettes representing a naked woman's body, known as 'a doctor's woman'. Sick women used to indicate on the statuette the part of their body which was causing them pain. We had seen statuettes of this sort several times in antique shops, some of them old and beautifully carved.

This explanation seemed to have cheered up Colette considerably. As for myself, still accompanied by the faithful and devoted Shu, I set off in search of a chemist. Shu stopped several times to ask passers-by for directions. I was happy wandering along these busy little streets all splashed with sunshine. On the corner of a wide avenue a chemist's shop came into sight, a haven of coolness and shade. Standing behind a dark wooden counter, two pale, sour-looking men reluctantly gave us a tube full of tiny white pills. I asked for three more, foreseeing a possible deterioration in the health of our little group. The walls of the shop were lined with oak shelves filled with coloured glass jars, as in old-fashioned English dispensaries. I started rummaging around as if I were in an antique shop, which was not at all to the liking of the two assistants.

On my return to the hotel, I discovered that Laure too was ill. She was sniffling, shivering and coughing. Madame Chapeau was still in bed and looking very pale. The prospects for the rest of the journey looked decidedly poor. And what was worse, it was my nicest companions who had fallen ill, as if laid low by malicious Chinese germs!

I took the survivors off to visit the Temple of the White Horse, dedicated to the monk Hsuan-Tsang, who, in the seventh century, under the T'ang dynasty, went off to India and brought back the writings of Buddha. He returned on a white palfrey and died as soon as he arrived home. Noiret, who was determined not to miss anything, asked if he could see the statue of the white horse, for he had read somewhere that one existed.

'Yes, where is the white horse?' repeated Signora Leandri.

'The white horse?' I said. 'I haven't the faintest idea. Shin, where is the white horse?'

Shin followed my example and swiftly passed the buck to his neighbour:

'The white horse? I don't know. Monsieur Pariet, where is the white horse?'

'There is no statue of the white horse,' declared Pariet, for once very well informed. 'It disappeared during one of your many civil wars.'

Hard luck, Pariet! There are some people who always manage to carry off bluffs like that, but not you. Your bluffs are shown up every time. Two days later, the statue of the white horse was to greet us in Sian Museum.

Fields speckled with snowy flakes of cotton stretched away to the foot of the blue hills in the distance. Standing on a wooden horse-drawn harrow, a huge herculean figure of a man appeared for a moment, stripped to the waist, with bulging muscles and a shaven head, driving his horse as if he were in a chariot race. It was strange to see this centaur-like creature, who looked as if he had descended from some Olympus, in the midst of a nation of ants. Before I had time to puzzle about him any longer, he had already disappeared. I shall never know how that man from another race had ended up in China. Wherever we looked, there were the same wooden ploughs drawn by half-a-dozen men, the same haggard, bent-backed men and women with vacant eyes, dragging the same carts piled high with cotton and bricks, the same peasant women bent double, picking cotton in groups of twenty, the same busy crowds and heavy traffic. Cyclists came so close they almost rode under the wheels of our coach which the driver was driving at top speed, sounding his horn arrogantly all the time. I shut my eyes in terror. Some poor women laboriously pushed their carts to the side of the road to get out of our way. On both sides human nature showed its irrepressible egoism in spite of Mao and his teachings...

Our next stop was a public park ablaze with flowers where two Han tombs had been reconstructed. They were discovered a few years ago by some workmen digging the foundations for a new railway line. To the delight of the archaeologists, similar discoveries have been made every time the Government has undertaken large-scale building projects. Almost every time a bridge, a dam, a railway or an apartment house has been built, the pickaxe of a Chinese labourer has turned up a bronze, a piece of ancient pottery or a statue. When that happens the local archaeological service is immediately alerted and comes along to assess the importance of the find on the spot. The Government has encouraged the formation of excellent teams of young archaeologists trained by scholars educated in American or European universities. Pariet told us that these teams had made some extraordinary finds, some of which were on display in Sian Museum, and which had rendered a few excellent studies on Chinese art inadequate or out-of-date. Unfortunately the Chinese publish only very incomplete reports on their excavations. When I expressed astonishment that tombs should have been moved from one place to another, Shin gently explained to me that 'it is easier for the people to come and see them in a public park than beside a railway track'. I saw his point. The park, like all Chinese gardens, was utterly delightful. The air was full of the scent of magnolias and wistarias, and hortensia blossoms decorated the trees with balls of colour. A little wooden bridge threw its graceful arch across a slow-moving river lit up by the reflection of a weeping willow.

This was a precious moment in which we were able to enjoy the poetry and serenity of Chinese Nature. We were strolling about in the peace of the gathering dusk when Georges Wolf suddenly seized hold of my hand. I was taken aback, for I had never dreamt that he had any particular feeling for me. Correctly, as it happened, for the only purpose of his gesture had been to slip into my clammy paw a tiny piece of the sculpture of one of the Han gates which he had found on the ground. I was delighted, and felt no remorse whatever at becoming a grave-robber.

My patients were still in a bad way. Laure, however, promised to get up to attend the dinner which the Government Delegation to Loyang were giving in our honour. The Head of the Delegation was a woman in her forties, dressed in the inevitable monastic trouser-suit, this time in dark grey gabardine. Short hair, a round face, beautiful firm features and a dazzling smile lent her a charm to which we were all immediately susceptible. She and I sat down beside each other, but once again, alas, the wretched language barrier confined us to the subjects of the Parisian climate and Chinese cooking. The system of the indispensable interpreter always proved paralysing whenever anybody tried to broach a remotely personal subject.

At the beginning of the dinner she stood up, followed by Shin, and delivered a speech on the usual themes: the friendship between our two peoples, and the hope that we had enjoyed our stay in Loyang, which, while a very old city, had also become a great industrial centre which was proud of its important tractor factory. Would we, she asked, care to 'correct their deficiencies'? Her humility did not irritate me. By now I knew this request by heart, but this woman struck me as being genuinely moved and thus very moving. I stood up in my turn, thanked her, and to my own surprise launched out into a lyrical little speech, likewise full of sincere emotion, in which I assured her of our interest, our friendship, and our admiration for all that they had achieved. Knowing the state of corruption and poverty which had existed before, we were amazed that China had been able to improve the lot of her people in so short a time, and that she had begun to solve the problems of food, housing, education, and economic development with such rapid results and without outside help. No doubt there still remained a long way to go, but we all hoped that this people we had begun to love would reach the end of that road without too much suffering. To my embarrassment, my companions burst into applause. Our hostess stood up and frantically shook both my hands. Shin murmured: 'Thank you, Madame, thank you.' As for Yuan, he came over to me, looked me in the eye, said: 'Kampei,' and emptied his glass at one gulp. I followed his example.

Dinner began. Fifteen exquisite dishes were served one after another by an army of mute waiters. Each of us had become accustomed to handling chopsticks and served himself straight from the dish. The little glasses of warm brownish wine followed in quick succession. Voices became louder and cheeks grew flushed. Laure stood up and made a charming little speech thanking the Chinese, Pariet and me. Noiret, who by now was as drunk as a lord, indulged in some subtle references to Marco Polo visiting Kublai Khan laden with gifts, whereas we had nothing to offer but our friendship. I privately doubted whether our hosts knew so much as the name of Kublai Khan. Then, to my alarm, Torti got to his feet, and made a few involved remarks about the renaissance of modern China, expressing the hope that she would take care not to go too far. I was horrified to see that Adrienne Mandois was now showing every intention of making her own little speech. Fearing the worst, I immediately brought the dinner to an end before Shin had even been able to translate Torti's remarks. There was nothing discourteous about my decision: the bowl of rice, the final dish which we were not supposed to touch, was already on the table. With supreme *savoir-faire*, the Chinese never linger at table after their banquets are over. Thank God.

# 12

The medical bulletin at eight o'clock in the morning on the platform of Loyang station was not very encouraging. Colette and Laure were pale and moribund, Madame Chapeau was shaken by fits of coughing, Madame Blum was depressed, and Georges Wolf was swathed in cashmere shawls like a mummy in bandages. Only the Italians were still in good shape. My dear Leandri slapped her thighs and explained:

'It's all the mao-tai I keep drinking that protects me against the Siberian virus.'

It had to be a Siberian virus, of course, which was responsible for everything, down to the pimple on Noiret's nose, for the more remote a thing is, the more exotic it seems. All the same, morale was not too bad, and the weather was warm and sunny. The train was clean and comfortable, or at least our carriages were—fortunately for us, for we were going to spend twelve hours in them! We settled down, four to a compartment, on bunks which remained permanently made up. To my delight, Colette, Laure and Madame Neralinda invited me to share their life, their compartment, and their germs. The train went past more loess hills, a landscape which would linger in my mind as one of the most characteristic scenes in China. I snuggled down under the soft floral eiderdown and went to sleep, following the example of my fever-ridden companions. In the other compartments the Italians were playing cards, the Blums and the Adjoufs chatting, Madame Chapeau knitting, and the rest reading. Towards the end of the morning the Musketeers came to keep us company, sitting on the lower bunks and telling us of their sentimental experiences. Dupont told us some wonderful jokes which kept us in fits of laughter. We drank pints of tea, and time went by, and the loess hills glided past like a slow-motion film outside the fish-bowl in which we were jolting up and down.

At one o'clock in the afternoon I led my party to the restaurant car through eight boneshaking carriages in which we found once more the traditional hierarchy of wooden benches, hard seats, and upholstered bunks with lace antimacassars. Every compartment was packed with people. Young men, soldiers, and whole families were sleeping, talking and playing cards, while mothers were nursing their babies. The passengers had arranged their tin plates and bowls on a shelf running along the corridor, above which hung dozens of white face-cloths. At each end of the carriage there was a washbasin and a spittoon.

In the restaurant car Colette and I sat side by side facing Adrienne Mandois and Shin. Adrienne treated us to a series of jokes in doubtful taste about Shin's probable or improbable sex life and what she imagined to be his abilities in that direction. Shin pretended not to hear, while we maintained a disapproving silence. Finally Colette lost patience and advised Adrienne to tackle Shin himself on the question. To our horror she promptly asked the poor man:

'Shin, have you ever been to bed with a woman?'

'No!' replied the crimson-faced Shin.

'How old are you?'

'Twenty-nine.'

'Then why haven't you slept with a woman?'

Shin was still red in the face, but he replied in a firm voice:

'Because that sort of thing isn't done in China any more when you aren't married. It was all right in the corrupt days of the previous régime.'

'You don't mean to tell me,' said Adrienne, 'that Chinese bachelors never make love?'

'Never. We are allowed to marry at thirty, and girls at twenty-five.'

'And what happens,' Adrienne asked, 'to the exception, the man who makes love even though he's a bachelor?'

'He is reprimanded. He has to make his autocriticism and marry the girl.'

Sticking to her prey like fly-paper, Adrienne went on:

'And what if he refuses to marry her?'

'Then that proves that he is not sufficiently familiar with the thoughts of Chairman Mao and needs re-educating.'

*Left:* In the first courtyard of the Imperial City in Peking stood a bronze crane. *Below:* Children spent their day off school sweeping the outer courtyards of the Imperial City with long-handled triangular straw brooms.

The Great Wall of China in which staircases, walls and paved slopes followed one another. In the distance the first of the Manchu Hills.

Next to the Summer Palace outside Peking, the Empress Tzu-Hsi built a boat o marble with funds misap propriated from the Navy

The Plain is crossed by a dead straight road lined on either side by a row of gigantic statues: dragons, elephants, tigers, hippopotami, horses and guards.

*Above:* Two girls in white bonnets weighing persimmons in wooden buckets placed on a weighing machine, just outside the Ming tombs. *Below:* In old Loyang a crowd gathered and followed us through the streets.

*Above:* Small school children in Loyang dressed in brightly coloured smocks looking like little bunches of flowers. *Below:* The reception squad.

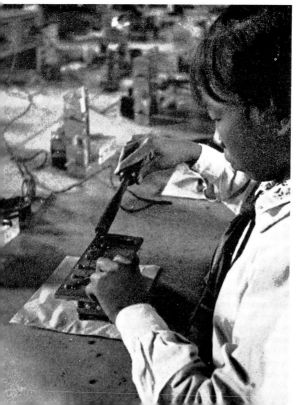

*Above:* The class-room. *Lef[t]*
In the school's radio wor[k]
shop each child was workin[g]
with the same intense co[n]
centration on his own litt[le]
transistor radio.

At Longmen, a serenely ironic Buddha, flanked by his grimacing guardians and a group of miniature Buddhas cut out of the grey-gold cliff.

The great hall of the Sian museum was full of huge stone statues, hieratic Buddhas in their stiff draperies.

*Above:* Hangchow: an agricultural commune. The hills were planted with tea shrubs and two girls imitated the tea-pickers for our cameras. *Below:* The commune was very pretty with white-washed brick houses covered with grey tiles. Girls were washing pots and pans in the small river.

*Above:* In a bamboo forest near Hangchow: the slim golden trees rose to a great height letting through rays of sunshine like dazzling arrows. *Below:* In the afternoon the sun gilded the lake in front of our hotel in Hangchow.

*Above:* On the banks of the lake men carted wooden buckets full of human manure: 'the brown gold' of China. *Below:* Women arriving for work in the rice fields outside Canton.

*Above:* Canton from the window of my hotel-room. *Left:* In an ivory workshop sixty men were cutting, chiselling blocks of ivory with the same accuracy as a Swiss watchmaker.

*Above:* We watched the children coming out of school. *Below:* The students watched with smiling, unashamed curiosity.

'Where?' asked Adrienne.

'Usually in an agricultural commune.'

I gently intervened to ask:

'Do you know a girl now, Shin, whom you would like to marry?'

Blushing furiously again—for in China personal questions are the height of indiscretion and not a sign of friendly interest—Shin replied:

'No, I haven't met such a girl yet.'

'What sort of girl do you think you would like to marry?' I asked. 'Would you like her to be pretty, intellectual, or what?'

'If she's pretty, so much the better, but above all she must be virtuous.'

Of course! I might have known that that would be his answer. Colette took up the questioning:

'Which is the virtue which strikes you as the most precious of all: honesty, charity, kindness, or what?'

Shin replied crisply:

'The thoughts of Chairman Mao.'

Taken aback, even annoyed, I said:

'Shin, that's going too far. What do you mean? Chairman Mao is a very great man. Nobody can deny that. But though his thoughts are the fruits of a mind of genius, they surely can't be classed as virtues, can they?'

'You are right, Madame,' came the reply, 'I express myself badly in French.' (A spot of autocriticism here!) 'What I meant was the virtue which leads us to follow the thoughts of Chairman Mao.'

He was sincere—that was obvious—even fervent, while I for my part was appalled. The man was a decent sort, and not at all stupid, so how could he and all his fellows sink into such fanatical obscurantism? No doubt this levelling of human thought was necessary to lift seven hundred million people out of the mud. The life of the mind was a luxury which could wait. When the material security of all had been assured, then it would be possible to start splitting hairs. But for the moment I was talking to one man, not seven hundred million—I was talking to my good friend Shin, and it was a painful experience.

'What would you like to do later on?' I asked him.

'I shall probably be a diplomat.'

'Is that what you want to be?'

'Yes, because that is the field in which I think I can best serve the people.'

'What career would you have chosen if you had followed your own inclination?'

Shin replied hesitantly:

'I would have liked to be an engineer.'

'Don't you feel any regret at having given up a scientific career?'

'No,' he said, 'since I am more useful to my country in other ways.'

'What does your father do?' I asked.

'Before the Liberation he was a diplomat. At present he is a professor at the School of Diplomatic Science in Peking.'

Now I understood Shin's physical distinction, his long hands and his good manners. His father, doubtless a member of the upper middle class, had probably welcomed the new régime hopefully, like many liberals and intellectuals, out of horror for the crimes and misery of the previous period. He had probably been asked to write a full and sincere history of his family and himself, a sort of genealogical autocriticism, which was quite in keeping with the Chinese tradition of consigning the life-story of the remotest relatives to tablets kept in the hall of ancestors. After careful study, his account had presumably been accepted as sincere, his faults judged to be venial, and he himself declared recoverable for the purpose of training new cadres. It is thanks to this system, of which Han Suyin has given some fascinating examples in her latest books, that China did not suffer from that chaotic intermediary period during which the absence of highly trained personnel has crippled the development of many young nations. So long as they were not guilty of crimes against the people, so long as they were innocent of murder, looting and oppression, many leading members of the upper middle class were 'recovered' in this way. So were many guilty men: a few war lords now occupy seats in the National Assembly. China has not hesitated to keep on certain factory owners as managers, and to use the services of scientists and doctors with bourgeois origins like Doctor Wong, pending the time when the new generation born of the people can take their place.

The landscape began to change. The line now ran between high plateaux covered with sparse undergrowth and split by narrow corridors. As we drew nearer to Sian, cultivated fields appeared and the trees became more numerous. Evening reddened the horizon which swiftly vanished into the golden mist.

# 13

I told myself that we were incredibly lucky to be treading the pale blue carpet and sitting in the comfortable armchairs of this beautiful red-painted pagoda. Incredibly lucky because this pagoda was nothing less than Sian station.

Sian, which for three centuries was the capital of the Ming emperors, is now the capital of that Shensi province which was the terminal point of the Long March, and where a little mountain town, Yenan, served as the headquarters of the Red Army. The Shensi province had consequently become the testing-ground for Maoism and later the 'new frontier' of the new China. In that mysterious province Sian is a mysterious town to which virtually no foreign travellers are allowed access. Only a few writers such as Edgar Snow, who devotes a chapter to it in his book *The Other Side of the River,* have enjoyed the privilege of visiting Sian since the Revolution. By what extraordinary favour were we there? I had no idea. We were the first ordinary visitors, and we should be the last for some time to come.

Under Chairman Mao's fatherly gaze the three local representatives of Luxingsche, the Chinese tourist agency, handed me our lodging vouchers, or to be more precise our room tickets, while my companions imbibed their twenty-fifth cup of tea of the day. We scrambled like schoolchildren aboard our Hungarian coach, and soon we were driving along the same narrow streets as in Loyang, with their small grey houses. But here, in this provincial capital, the roofs were covered with shining yellow tiles and the ridges were turned up and decorated with delicate statues of dragons, horsemen, soldiers and lions. After the superb red and gold columns of the Ming belfries, the coach drove past the splendidly restored Ming ramparts, flanked by the four towers which ensured the protection of the old capital. Bursting out *extra muros*, the modern town revealed broad avenues, three or four-storeyed apartment buildings, shopping centres and factories. Adrienne yawned and clamoured for an apple.

'You don't get enough vitamins in this damned country,' she groaned.

The coach stopped in the old town, and we were immediately surrounded by a smiling crowd. Pariet, who was now used to this sort of thing, trotted out a pretty little speech in Chinese. It was a triumph. The crowd grew thicker every moment. The slightest remark drew a roar of laughter and applause. We were a little intoxicated by it all, but Shin put an end to our popular success by dragging us off to our hotel. A few grumbles were heard on the way.

'What sort of dump are we going to find in a town where there are never any tourists?' asked Signora Leandri, who was beginning to find China 'a little prrrimitive'.

To our surprise the hotel was a large modern building put up in the fifties to accommodate Russian technicians and their families. Each bedroom had an adjoining sitting-room with deep armchairs, writing-paper and the inevitable giant thermos flask full of hot water next to a canister of green tea. In the bathroom I was met by the familiar tar-like smell of the rather rough pink soap provided by Chinese hotels. The service was excellent. In no time at all the luggage had been taken up to our rooms, and for once everybody seemed delighted.

In accordance with a now unchangeable ritual Yuan, Shin, Shu and I met for a preliminary conference with the three local tourist agents. The latter presented us with the programme of festivities they had drawn up. We drank some tea and I handed round cigarettes (an American brand). I praised the achievements of the People's Government, spoke warmly of the friendship with which we were always greeted, and stressed the great interest Sian had for us. I went on to say that I was therefore counting on our hosts' boundless understanding to allow us one or two minor changes in the programme. A visit to a temple instead of a factory, for example. I explained that there were a few artlovers in our party who would be delighted by such a favour. I also explained that our common aim remained the success of the tour for the greater benefit of the community. I had become very 'Chinese'. I never spoke any more about 'individuals' but always about the 'community'. Shin translated my words with genuine sympathy, lending support to what I had said, as I could tell from the tone of his voice. The local agents consulted together. Finally they agreed to my request. I thanked them effusively, and after countless handshakes I went off to collapse into a hot bath, after washing my lingerie, mending the hem of my only skirt and resewing the buttons of my jacket which was so tired it was beginning to lose its shape.

The dining-room looked like the restaurant of a grand hotel with its big round tables and immaculate tablecloths. We had hardly sat down before Boilèle started complaining about the delicious food, copied straight away by the grousers in our party. I accordingly decided to institute two tables: a 'European table' and a 'Chinese table'. Henceforth each person would sit down at one or other of these tables, according to his taste in food, and refrain from all recrimination. I lost no time in taking my place at the Chinese table, fleeing the company of the steak-and-chips brigade forever. I was promptly followed by all the friendly members of the party. Indeed, all those who were prepared to contribute more to the journey than a suit-case rushed to join the Chinese table, which would always be the livelier and more amusing of the two.

The next morning, about seven o'clock, a ray of sunshine filtering between the heavy brown velvet curtains forced me to open one eye. I opened the other thanks to my usual precious cup of Nescafé. My room overlooked a huge square of beaten earth. In the middle, the ground was marked with white circles and some young men in track-suits were running between the lines. The whole square was speckled with little figures doing slow physical training movements punctuated by the whistle blasts which had disturbed my last hour of sleep. On the right was a huge big top: there was obviously a circus in town. I thought how fascinating it would be to see a Chinese circus— their acrobats were supposed to be quite extraordinary—and I resolved to try to change the visit to the opera planned for that evening into a visit to the circus.

The great attraction of the day was to be a visit to the T'ang tombs about forty miles outside Sian, where we were looking forward to seeing the famous frescoes depicting Wu-Tai, an unfortunate empress who had her hands and feet chopped off and her son strangled on the orders of her emperor husband, who was himself acting at the instigation of the cruel concubine Tsan Woo-ti. The frescoes depict the empress's daily life and are a unique example of eighth-century Chinese painting. This visit to the T'ang tombs was supposed to be one of the high spots of the tour, and the Curator of the Cernuschi Museum had asked Laure and me to bring back some photographs of them, for there were no reproductions of either tombs or frescoes in existence.

I had naturally taken care to obtain confirmation of the excursion as soon as I arrived. Hence the violent cramp that twisted my long-suffering stomach when I saw Shin's expression as he came rushing over to me.

'We are terribly sorry, Madame Modiano,' he said, 'but we shan't be able to visit the T'ang tombs this morning.'

Tense with suppressed fury, I asked:

'Then when shall we be able to visit them, my dear Shin?'

'Never, I'm afraid,' he answered sheepishly. 'We shan't be able to visit them at all.'

'And why not, if I may ask?'

'The road is very bad. There has been a lot of rain recently.'

'Was the road any better last night,' I asked, 'when we worked out our programme together?'

'I'm afraid not,' said Shin. 'In any case, it's very bad today.'

'Is there any chance it might be better tomorrow,' I inquired, 'if the rain stops?'

'I don't think so,' was the firm reply. 'There are workers resurfacing the road.'

'We don't mind an uncomfortable journey,' I pointed out, 'provided we see the frescoes.'

'We are terribly sorry, Madame Modiano, but we simply can't go there. The road is very bad and we cannot possibly take you along bad roads.'

And that was that. I gave a sigh of exasperation. Shin gave a sigh of embarrassment. We looked at each other and I gave him a pale little smile. Neither of us could do a thing to change the situation.

The reception I got from my little party, wrapped in its raincoats and bristling with umbrellas like a giant porcupine, was as cool as the weather.

Laure exclaimed: 'My dear, that's impossible. You've simply got to *do* something.'

Colette grumbled between two fits of coughing: 'Are you sure there's nothing to be done?'

Noiret snarled angrily: 'It's disgusting. These people seem quite incapable of honouring their obligations.'

Monsieur Chapeau murmured sadly: 'What a pity!'

Madame Adjouf stated objectively: 'It's very disappointing.'

General de Boilèle howled: 'It's a scandal! I shall complain to your office in Paris!'

And Madame Trollan sneered: 'I shall demand a refund for part of the tour. This is disgraceful. If you were at all conscientious you would take steps to remedy the situation.'

There was such a hubbub that I might have been in the National Assembly—the French one, of course—if it weren't for the fact that there were no desk lids being banged. This was one of the moments a sensitive tour courier enjoys most of all.

With a rather shrill edge to my voice, I asked my party to get into the coach which was going to take us to the Shensi provincial museum.

It was raining cats and dogs. The beaten earth of Circus Square was an absolute quagmire, studded with deep, soggy puddles. Nothing could have been more depressing, and it was in a sinister silence that we left the old city.

'I don't suppose we'll see the Pagoda of the Drum either?' snarled Boilèle from the back of the coach.

'You are right as usual,' I replied. 'The Pagoda of the Drum has been taken over to be used as Government offices.'

But sarcasm didn't help. I looked out glumly at the roofs glistening in the rain, and I felt tired; tired of my tourists, and the imperturbable good humour and constant attention they demanded from me, tired of the Chinese, and the perpetual tact and artificial language the simplest dealings with them required, tired of this strange country which was so fascinating and so inaccessible to foreigners of good will, tired too of trailing around for twelve days in the same suit which was beginning to smell like a wet dog, and especially tired of my untidy mop which was beginning to show the lack of a hairdresser's attention. In short, I was a poor, tired, lonely little woman, feeling very sorry for herself. Sitting behind my dark glasses, with a cigarette in my moist, trembling little hand, I felt tears pricking my eyes. I could still hear grumbling going on behind me. Signora Negri was arguing in her vinegary voice with her daughter, Isabella, who retorted that it wasn't my fault and that I probably couldn't do whatever I liked in China. (She could say that again!) I breathed a silent thank you to dear, gay Isabella.

It was a bad-tempered coach-load that I disembarked at the Museum, a former temple of Confucius which consisted of a succession of graceful red octagonal pagodas with varnished roofs, separated by paved courtyards planted with trees and flowers. The atmosphere was peaceful and poetic. Raindrops were sparkling on hosts of roses. The sun was beginning to shine and the general tranquillity affected us all. From the tip of the ridge tiles of each pagoda hung a little bell which gave a silvery tinkle in the slightest breeze.

In the pagoda which contained the latest archaeological discoveries we all held our breaths: the great hall lit by frosted glass windows was full of huge stone statues, hieratic Han Buddhas in their stiff draperies, fourth-century Wei tigers in strong relief, and huge Chou bronze vases from the tenth century B.C. I stopped in admiration in front of two high reliefs in marble from the T'ang tombs to which we had been forbidden access. Each depicted a galloping horse, and they stood next to two motionless horses. The latter were just plaster casts, Shin whispered to me: 'The originals were stolen by the Americans and are now in Philadelphia.'

Whole pagodas were filled with Chou vases as big as the bells of Notre-Dame, and others with showcases crowded with camels, cameleers, soldiers, favourites and dancers in T'ang pottery. Boilèle started shouting again, but this time with joy:

'This is so beautiful I feel like crying!'

Once again he awakened a brief spark of sympathy in me, though heaven knows ... The exhibits were interspersed with realistic models showing the various peasant revolts of China, so that nobody should forget that these masterpieces were due to the victories of the people. We then went through the so-called 'sea of steles', tall slabs of black granite engraved with drawings and historical inscriptions. One of them bore a Nestorian inscription: the Nestorians, Pariet informed me in a whisper, were Byzantine Christians who established themselves in China in the seventh century. I found the 'sea of steles' rather boring and went back to the displays of statues and bronzes. Our party had broken up and was scattered among the various rooms. Some were taking photographs or films, others simply uttering oohs and ahs: everybody was fascinated and happy. The Chinese had disappeared, bored to tears and quite unable to appreciate what Shin called 'these old things'. We ourselves were in fact the only people in this remarkable yet almost unknown museum.

Going back one last time to see the Wei tiger and fix it in my memory, I noticed a wooden hut tucked away among the trees. The door was standing ajar. Inquisitive as ever, I peeped inside and found four tall wooden crates leaning against the wall. A little farther on were three more cases which were open. It was rather dark inside the hut and I am short-sighted. There was nobody outside. I boldly went in.

To my amazement, there before me were the frescoes from the T'ang tombs! There was Wu-Tai, the tragic empress, still possessed, thank heaven, of her hands and feet, and with her hair piled high on her head. Dressed in a long pink gown, she stood before me, surrounded by her ladies in waiting. And scattered pell-mell on a nearby work-bench were T'ang horses and vases which had been found in the same tomb.

I felt like Alice in Wonderland. Alone in that world outside time, I gazed at Wu-Tai as if the thirteen centuries which separated us had vanished. So this was the explanation of the bad road: since the tombs had been emptied of their treasures and the frescoes were no longer there, there was no longer any reason to go and visit them. But in that case, why all the mystery? With very little contact between the various Chinese Government departments, the officials in charge of tourism probably didn't know themselves that the frescoes were in the museum. Then why the lie about the road? The answer would seem to be that they had to tell a lie out of politeness towards their foreign guests and to save face themselves. That sort of thing infuriates Westerners, who have a passion for truth—by which they naturally mean their own truth—and find it difficult to understand the lies which go to make 'politeness', that code which nobody is expected to believe. It is our notion of credibility which invalidates all our relations with Orientals. The Chinese wrap up their yeses and noes—especially their noes—in more or less plausible stories, as a matter of courtesy and consideration, just as we wrap up our Christmas presents in pretty coloured paper.

I went rushing around looking for Shin and hung on to his coat-tails until he begged Yuan to give me permission to take my party to the hut. There was a long confabulation with the museum officials. Then Shin smiled: 'Yes.' The news was greeted rapturously by my companions. This, I decided, was my lucky day...

# 14

The usual everyday problems were waiting for me on my return. Colette was still bronchitic and Madame Chapeau white-faced, Laure feverish, and Georges suffering from a cold, Noiret had an eye infection and looked like an albino rabbit, while Adrienne was still complaining of the same old tummy trouble. Madame Blum, who had a heavy cold, kept making uncharitable remarks about the Italians, who seemed proof against germs and impervious to epidemics.

In the afternoon, nobody showed any enthusiasm for the scheduled visit to a textile mill. But there was no question of skipping it, for I could tell that Yuan was very keen on it and if I wanted to obtain a second visit to the museum...

On each side of the entrance to the mill, large wooden hoardings like those you see in France in an election campaign were covered with red and yellow posters. These were the 'public newspapers'.

After a brief stop in the reception room, the manager informed us that the mill employed 6,000 workers, possessed 3,200 looms and produced 300,000 yards of material a day.

I hung on to the arm of Monsieur Chapeau whom I wanted to act as the factory guide. A gleam came into his blue eyes as soon as we entered the first workshop, where a few workers were standing behind the machines. Most of the looms were working unattended. The women were dressed in faded cotton trousers, which were patched but clean, and light-coloured blouses, with their hair protected by white headscarfs. The men, in overalls or singlets, were sweating in the tremendous heat. We were not spared a single stage in the manufacturing process, from the bales of raw cotton to the final rolls of material. Monsieur Chapeau remarked to me:

'I've never seen such huge workshops before. And it's all very clean. I gather there are very few looms out of action here. In France there are always more looms out of action—at least four per cent. But one thing surprises me: the absence of any dust extractors.'

Most of the workers did in fact have a gauze mask over their nose and mouth. As for us, unmasked and unprotected, we sneezed and spat our way through the mill. As we walked along, Monsieur Chapeau pointed out an English loom to us, then several Russian looms, and finally a Chinese machine.

On the walls of a corridor between two of the workshops there were some brightly coloured posters illustrating the commandments of the Maoist dogma. They depicted a dear little Chinese with an intelligent face and mischievous eyes—a local version of Tintin, in fact—whose actions suggested that his fellow countrymen should wash, work, lead honest lives, exercise daily, go into training to defend China against attack, and first of all, above all, and most important of all, know by heart the thoughts of Chairman Mao, thanks to which Shin-Tintin and his fellow countrymen would be able to follow all the previous recommendations.

At the foot of a staircase leading to the despatch department, I found myself face to face with the Chinese concept of the 'Wicked American', an odious creature with a pale face, a long hooked nose, and red-rimmed eyes (probably due to his indulgence in all the vices). He was being dragged in the mud by magnificent specimens of those peoples which were fighting for their liberty: a Cuban, an African, an Arab, a Vietnamese, and finally an individual who looked like the late lamented Rubirosa, probably a Brazilian or a Bolivian. However good the cause, this sort of crude propaganda, appealing above all to instincts of hatred, is intensely irritating. Standing in front of these posters, I recalled the faces of a few dear American friends, and I also remembered the German posters during the Occupation which depicted the Jews as monstrous and ridiculous; and although I stand fairly solidly for freedom and for peace in Vietnam and elsewhere, I felt annoyed. But then I reflected that there was probably no other means of stirring a huge and largely illiterate people except by these crude methods.

When I am thinking, I look either sad or stupid. This time I must have been looking stupid, for the factory guide came up to me and explained:

'Americans beaten by world coalition.'

Thanks, old man, I muttered. I felt I had enough of all this—these confabulations, this humourless officialdom, this dogmatic rule of life, this self-righteous lyricism. Oh, for a bit of downright cynicism! I missed the laughter of France, and the irony too. I turned my eyes away from the poor Wicked American, who was having a hard time of it, and thoughtfully made my way back through the workshops alone. I immediately found myself being recaptured by my own China, and felt a wave of affection well up inside me at the sight of these smooth-faced women who smiled at me and came to look at my clothes. The men, though more distant and indifferent, were moving too. They worked so very hard. They had come so far, out of a world of poverty, death, hunger and disease, and their life was still so precarious and hard. It was not pity I felt, but sympathy, and there is never any point in explaining feelings. In spite of occasional irritation—the irritation of a spoilt liberal—I liked this country I didn't know and these people I couldn't talk to. The workers in this mill looked healthy and well fed, and my good humour had returned. I was joking happily as I led my companions in the rain towards the fabric-printing workshop which was in the next street.

At the entrance the same newspapers were posted up on hoardings. At Peking one day, I had had a chance to read an English edition of one of these papers. There was nothing in it except for news of provincial delegations visiting the capital, a banquet presided over by Chou En-lai, and the prowess of star-worker Tse Tu-tai in swimming across the Yangtse Kiang. No foreign news whatever, unless you counted the departure of a delegation of Chinese workers for Pakistan.

After a fresh encounter with a picture of a dirty white exploiter of the human race, I learnt that all the machines in the mill had been made in China and that the workshops were air-conditioned. A model of urbanity, the manager brought us together for the usual cup of green tea under the portraits of Engels, Lenin, Marx, Mao and six other Chinese whose faces meant nothing to me. He treated us to a long speech which some of my well bred companions punctuated with frequent yawns. Lodgings had been provided, he explained, for both families and unmarried workers, around the mill, as well as a library, sports facilities, schools, crèches, kindergartens, and also a park.

'Favourable circumstances,' he added, 'have enabled us to achieve a considerable improvement in the quality of our products.' I could see what was coming, and sure enough here it came: 'We have overcome all obstacles, thanks to the thoughts of Chairman Mao.' He went on: 'By the authority of the Chinese Communist Party we are going to launch a campaign for young pioneers and we intend to go even further. We are determined to support the struggle for freedom of the Vietnamese people and all the peoples of the world thanks to ...' I listened eagerly for what was coming ... 'thanks to the quality of our excellent products.'

And that was that! Those who had been listening looked absolutely hypnotized, while those who were dozing were oblivious of what was being said, Shin's mumbled translation failing to reach either heart, mind or eardrum.

The whole visit had been very convincing. Even Chapeau was unstinting in his praise. I tugged at his sleeve and said:

'Ask the manager some questions.'

Then there followed a conversation which might have been between two deaf men, the answers bore so little relation to the questions.

*Chapeau:* 'How many printing machines have you got?'

*The Manager:* 'What matters is not the number of machines, but the total output.'

*Chapeau* (imperturbably): 'Do you use the automatic frame technique?'

*The Manager:* 'We have no automatic frames, but we have assembly line production.'

*Chapeau:* 'Are your frames operated by hand?'

*The Manager:* 'Our materials are printed in an assembly line.'

*Chapeau:* 'Are your machines equipped with copper rollers?'

*The Manager:* 'That is difficult to explain. We shall see.'

*Chapeau:* 'Are the dyes you use imported or produced in China?'

*The Manager:* 'The raw material is produced in China.'

I got the impression that our worthy guide was no more the manager of his mill than I was an acrobat, and that his duties were more concerned with spreading the thoughts of Chairman Mao than with printing fabrics.

Leaving the building and crossing a large open space which served as a sports ground, we entered an apartment house. I climbed a narrow cement staircase which led up to the door of a room twelve feet long containing a washbasin and four beds, with a floral eiderdown folded in four at the foot of each bed. Four girls greeted me with smiles and little gestures of welcome and asked me to sit down on one of the beds. The white paint or the walls was flaking off. The room had two calligraphed posters, which looked to my eyes like abstract paintings. It was clean and austere, but it obviously seemed very comfortable to these girls who had probably never known what it was to have electricity or running water before. Naturally most of my companions sneered at what they saw, and I wondered how many of them had ever set foot in a working-class house in their own country. In spite of good intentions on both sides the conversation was fragmentary to say the least, and went no further than an exchange of smiles and gestures. My four round-faced hostesses escorted me to the door of the apartment building where they gathered around me, imitated by their friends, who examined me minutely with benevolent curiosity, indicating and touching each article of my clothing in turn. As usual, it was my shoes and stockings which interested them most. There was no mockery in their behaviour: they were smiling and even friendly. One of them, taller than the rest, had an elegant bearing and beautiful delicate features. Where did she come from? What was her story? Another human life I had to pass by because of lack of time and the impossibility of communication.

A loud burst of applause came from inside the big top. As I was bringing up the rear of the party, and was still outside in the rain, I assumed that the show had already started. I was wrong: it was Boilèle whom the circus audience was applauding —Boilèle who was proudly leading the way, delightedly lifting his chin in the air like a real Duce. Each member of the party had his share of the applause which only stopped when the last of us, in other words myself, had sat down. It was ironically amusing to have all those faces smiling at us, all those calloused hands applauding us, when most of us were ripe examples of reactionary capitalism and all of us, in any case, were well-to-do bourgeois. It made you feel slightly ashamed. You almost felt like telling those people whose lives were nothing but work, zeal, privations and hope that there had been a misunderstanding, that we were not 'relatives of Uncle Mao', and that there were no more than two or three among us who liked them or even wanted to understand them. Be that as it may, it was something of a thrill to be applauded by a crowd and surrounded by smiles, even if the reasons for these marks of interest had nothing to do with our personal merits.

There, in that Chinese big top, for the first time in my life, and probably the last, I understood the intoxication of fame.

Sitting on wooden chairs, poorly dressed, with their feet on the beaten earth, the audience seemed to be largely composed of workers and peasants. Their dark grey or blue clothes were sometimes patched or darned, always clean, their faces drawn with fatigue, their eyes weary, their bodies often bent by hard work and insufficient food. There were some young men and women but a great many middle-aged people with deeply wrinkled faces, whole families of sleeping children, and grandmothers with bound feet and black tunics rocking them in their arms. Everybody was silently nibbling apples, nuts, little cakes, peanuts and sesame seeds. They kept turning round to smile at us, leaning to one side to get a better view of us.

The show began with a roll of drums and a clash of cymbals. The various numbers followed one another in dizzy succession —animal trainers, cyclists, and acrobats as light as a feather, as quick as lightning and as graceful as sprites. The light-hearted humour of the show and a witty fantasy unusual in China filled us with delight. Even the clowns, whom I always find boring or sinister, were funny. The men's costumes were covered with sparkling sequins, while the girls were dressed in light-coloured silk pyjamas. Their gestures were lively and feminine. I had stopped expecting to find any grace, fantasy or humour in the austere workaday atmosphere of modern China.

We applauded frantically. The delighted audience looked at us, smiled with pleasure at our enthusiasm, and clapped louder than ever.

At a roll on the drums the sprites skipped out of the ring. Another roll on the drums brought an indefinable change of atmosphere. One of those pale-faced creatures with a long nose and red-rimmed eyes like the 'Wicked American' on the poster leapt into the ring. He was wearing a G.I. uniform and brandishing a fistful of dollars. Along came a Chinese worker dressed in blue who struck the G.I. with the back of his hand and sent his banknotes flying. Then, in the course of a painful pantomime, he proceeded to beat up the American, who bit the dust (in this case the sawdust). The spectators in front of us turned round and looked at us, this time without smiling, inquisitively but not aggressively. They applauded. We remained as cold as ice and didn't move a muscle. Yuan, Shin and Shu didn't applaud either. A trio of women acrobats then bounced into the ring and eased the atmosphere. Dressed in gaily rustling pyjamas, they all wore lipstick, had long shining hair, and displayed the most amazing dexterity and courage.

Apart from the number about the G.I., with its vulgar and —whatever one's personal opinions—distressing brutality, this show put on by a little circus in a little provincial town was a thousand times better than any performance under a Western big top, thanks to its incomparable virtuosity, elegance and originality.

When it was over, I came out with the slow-moving crowd, and I hopped and skipped from puddle to puddle all the way to the hotel.

# 15

Rain was pouring from the low grey sky and lashed my face when I opened the curtains in the morning. With our raincoats, boots and umbrellas, we looked like a battalion of surface divers. I was proudly brandishing a spinach-green brolly I had bought in Loyang. It sprang out of its handle like a flick-knife at the slightest pressure from my finger, and gave me in my luggage-less condition the comforting feeling that I possessed something at least. Completely deserted for mile after mile, the slushy countryside had been turned brown by the wet soil, the precious loess of China. In the muddy village streets a few peasants in black rubber capes were wearing boots. The rest were paddling about in their usual felt slippers.

We had travelled four thousand years into the past. It was in 1953 that a Chinese labourer discovered the Neolithic village of Pan-Po. Thinking that his pickaxe had unearthed the remains of a tomb, he obeyed the instructions given to all workers in such a case and informed the foreman in charge of the building site, who in turn alerted the archaeological service. The result was the excavation of two thousand square yards of a town covering five acres, where it is now possible to see the lines of the streets and the circular or square foundations of the houses. The remains have been covered with a huge glass roof, a device which struck us as doubly brilliant in that driving rain.

The archaeologists had surrounded their excavations with a sort of balcony overlooking them. We gazed thoughtfully or absentmindedly at the walls of these houses in which human beings had lived four thousand years ago. It occurred to me that we were just as unreal as they were in the eyes of someone like Shin, for example, always supposing that Shin could ever think of anything but following the wonderful thoughts of Chairman Mao.

On the whole my Martians didn't seem to find the excavations either thrilling or thoughtprovoking. They were feeling chilly and grumpily made their way back to the coach. As usual, it was the Blums, Georges, Chapeau, Claire Adjouf and a sneeze-shaken Laure who formed a thoughtful little rearguard on the balcony. Pariet told us that the T'angs had begun excavations in China as far back as the tenth century. In 1920 some French archaeologists resumed the work which had been abandoned for a thousand years, pirating some of their finds. Abandoned once more in 1937 on account of the Japanese invasion, the excavations only started again in 1950, on the initiative of the new régime. Scholars trained in the United States and Europe trained young archaeologists in their turn at Peking University. At the moment, Pariet explained, China was studded with ex-cavation sites which were yielding up a host of historical and artistic treasures, some of which could be seen in Sian Museum. Unfortunately, he added, the Chinese cast a veil of secrecy over most of their finds.

From my observation point I noticed the beautiful Isabella still flirting with Shin, walking beside him, fluttering her eye-lashes, and talking softly to him. Poor, chaste Shin was growing redder and redder, deeply disturbed but utterly delighted.

In spite of the rain, Shin insisted on taking us to see the hot springs at Wa-Shin-She, where, Tsan Woo-ti, the rival of the poor Empress Wu-Tai, the one who had her hands and feet cut off, was fond of taking the waters with her imperial lover. A series of pagodas clung to a hill from which willows wept into an artificial lake covered with dead leaves splashed with large drops of rain. Rose petals kept drifting down on to the sodden ground, and the sky was leaden. Chilled to the marrow, we crossed an arched bridge and entered the Favourite's pagoda, which was furnished with the sort of bed and dressing-table the visitor to an elegant spa would expect.

Without the slightest warning we suddenly jumped a thous-and years: before us was the pagoda from which Chiang Kai-shek fled to the mountains in the middle of the night, dressed only in his pyjamas, and in his haste leaving behind his false teeth and his glasses on his bedside table. This was in the famous night of the Sian Incident of 12 December 1936 during which one of the Generalissimo's former companions, General Chang Hsueh-liang, who had recently rallied to Mao's cause, had come to arrest him. We were shown his hard, narrow bed, and we slipped and slithered in the mud as far as the place where they had found him at the foot of a tree. It was all rather sinister. Then, right out of the blue, Shin suggested that we might like a bath in the hot springs. Brrr. We all declined the kind offer in unison, and returned shivering with cold.

A long confabulation with Yuan to try to swap a visit to the local military academy for another visit to the museum. I finally got my way, to the general joy of my pilgrims, who clearly found the past more attractive than the present.

The afternoon found us all together under the corrugated iron roof of a little market. A host of little stalls displaying gimcrack treasures: scissors shaped like butterflies' wings, oval wooden combs decorated with pen-and-ink drawings of pagodas or junks, and umbrellas and parasols in varnished straw made of strips of wood and oiled parchment. At the far end of the market there was an unusual shop-window containing two black wigs, a pith helmet, and a British naval officer's cap. It was a theatrical costumier's, a small square shop, with 'Imperialist uniforms' stacked in piles reaching up to the ceiling, Chinese costumes of the *ancien régime* for landowners and mandarins, long women's dresses in silk, more wigs, false beards and moustaches, rubber machine-guns and wooden pistols. Within a few seconds the shop was full of the joyful din of shouts and laughter. Boilèle in a false beard looked more like a 'Wicked Imperialist' than ever. I bought a pair of royal blue silk pyjamas with wide trouser-legs, like those the acrobats had worn at the circus. Signora Coli chose a pair in turquoise, and Isabella a mustard-coloured pair. The stallkeeper was at once petrified and overjoyed: business was booming, but what queer customers we were! He obviously thought we were 'friends of Chairman Mao', but rather crazy friends judging by the frenzy with which we were buying up his stock. Shu laughingly confided to me that the good man had finally decided that we must be a troupe of actors.

I quietly slipped away in the hope of being able to go for a stroll by myself in the streets of Sian. To my surprise, the shopkeepers called out to me and beckoned me to come and look at their wares, whereas they always showed a hieratic reserve when we were in a group and accompanied by our interpreters. I went up to them and they spoke to me, laughing and joking.

As soon as I left the main avenue, I found myself wading in the mud of narrow streets lined with huts. Through the open doors I caught glimpses of cramped, squalid rooms with about a dozen people in each. At that time of day I could see only old people and children, the former looking after the latter. There were a great many old women in black tunics, with bound feet. This was still yesterday's China.

When I got back to the coach, I found Shin with his forehead furrowed by a frown.

'Where have you been?' he asked. 'I was worried about you.'

'Oh, come now, Shin,' I said with a smile. 'I'm in no danger here.'

I decided to play fair with him and told him about my incursion into the China of dirt and poverty, the China which had so far been hidden from us. Rather annoyed, he carefully explained that twenty years ago the whole of China had been like the sordid streets I had just walked through and that it had been impossible to get rid of them all in seventeen years. That was fair enough. The government, he added solemnly, was faced with a gigantic housing problem and it was natural that the first to benefit should be the young, both married and unmarried, since they were the life and strength of the country. It was therefore the young who had to be provided with decent living conditions before anyone else, to enable them to achieve the maximum improvement in their productive efficiency.

From the top of a tower dominating a rectangular Ming pagoda with a triple roof of green tiles, I later looked down on to the maze of alley-ways I had barely glimpsed in the course of my solitary escapade. The peasants' big round straw hats looked like water-lilies floating on the grey surface of a lake. A fugitive, frozen vision of eternal China, faraway China, the China of my childhood dreams. I spared a smile for those childhood dreams, of course, but above all for that sweet, exotic picture of China which the China of today, with its ruthless efficiency and determination, would, I felt sure, never efface. For I believed that that sweetness, that grey harmony, was also part of China.

The director of the Sian tourist service, Madame Li, gave us a dinner of sixteen courses accompanied by speeches and toasts. By now I knew the routine, and the words came tripping off my tongue. My audience was excellent and applauded everything. Madame Li was a beautiful woman, in spite of her hair, which looked as if it had been cut with a pruning-knife, and her grey gabardine suit. Her face was strong and noble, her smile dazzling, her eyes bold. I felt a little sad at being unable to question this forty-year-old woman about her origins, her past, her opinions. But as soon as I asked a question which was at all personal in nature, the interpreter turned the conversation in another direction. The only questions that were translated were those about the weather, our itinerary, French and Chinese food, and of course, our hosts' 'weaknesses and deficiencies'.

# 16

Crossing the red carpet of the pretty lacquered station, we returned to our eiderdowned compartment and were soon looking out again at the traditional landscape of loess hills which in the rain looked like huge sand castles attacked by the rising tide. We had twenty-six hours of travelling to look forward to, and there was a general feeling of torpor. The Siberian virus had gained ground. The previous day Adrienne had told me that she felt very ill and that she simply had to have a compartment all to herself. Accustomed to the diplomatic character of her ailments, I refused point blank. According to Torti, my companions then laid bets as to which of us would win. I was absolutely determined not to give way. I told the Chinese that I was opposed to Adrienne's demands, which struck me as contrary not only to their socialist community spirit, but also to the rules of good behaviour in the West. I maliciously stressed the unexpected character of this identity of views. There was no visible reaction.

A few moments after the train had left the station, I noticed Adrienne whispering in Shin's ear. Ten minutes later, installed in a compartment of her own, she was looking me up and down with triumphant disdain.

Beside myself with rage, I promptly got hold of Shu.

'Where are you sleeping tonight, Shu? Here?'

'No, Madame,' she replied. 'I've got a seat in the next compartment.'

'My dear Shu,' I said, 'I must apologize for the chore I'm going to inflict on you, but I'd be grateful if you would share the compartment of Madame Mandois, who isn't feeling very well. Besides, it strikes me as rather embarrassing for her with regard to her companions, to have a whole compartment all to herself.'

The others in my compartment, Laure, Colette and Madame Neralinda, were delighted and clucked with joy at having won their bet, even if I had cheated a little. We sank into a deep sleep. I in my turn was beginning to feel lightheaded and hoarse.

The loess hills were followed by fields of corn and maize, and then by paddyfields. Not a single road, not a single car, not a single lorry. A few mud tracks, and carts drawn by men: there were obviously fewer draught animals here than in the north. Time went by, warmer and stickier the farther we travelled towards the south-east. We barricaded the door of our compartment to avoid being woken up with a start by the teapot comrade. Chinese trains travel so slowly that it is easy to sleep and read on them. You can also talk, which isn't necessarily an advantage. I could unfortunately hear the conversations in the next compartments through the partitions. Pariet was deep in a political argument with Shu. In spite of my earplugs, his idealistic socialism struck me as incompatible with the thoughts of Chairman Mao. Pariet got excited and started shouting. I heard Shin's hesitant voice, which I couldn't quite make out, and when Pariet started shouting again I banged hard on the wall.

Dragging myself to the restaurant car later, I found myself sharing a table with Adrienne, Noiret and Shin. Adrienne embarked on another of her grillings.

'Shin, what is your ambition in life?'

As was to be expected, Shin had no ambition.

'Come now, Shin, what would you like to do?'

Again as was to be expected, Shin wanted nothing better than to serve the people.

'Shin, drop the propaganda!'

Predictable as ever, Shin declared that what he had said was the truth and not propaganda. I, who knew that Shin was going into the diplomatic service in spite of his desire to be an engineer, thought to myself that he had made a wise choice. His air of distinction and his charming manners would be sure to correct the Western picture of the Chinese Communist with a knife between his teeth and an H-bomb in his pocket!

Deciding that she had teased Shin enough, Adrienne turned her attention to Noiret who, overwhelmed by the honour, puffed out his little chest and pointed his nose towards the paddyfields. A Dior dress cost five thousand francs nowadays. It was really impossible. Like a Chanel suit, you know. A passing reference to the Rothschilds, who had done nothing to deserve it. Then Noiret dazzled even himself with what must have been an exhaustive account of all the châteaux he knew and the cost of keeping them up. Shin listened open-mouthed to this music-hall sketch which far outdid all the anti-capitalist propaganda he could ever have ingurgitated. I could feel my toes curling in exasperation and shame.


After absorbing a vast number of multicoloured pills with various desirable effects, we wished one another a good night's sleep, and I slipped delightedly into my silky acrobat's pyjamas (I had already returned Georges Wolf's wonderful blue Sulka pyjamas to their owner, completely faded by the Sian laundry). A restless, sweating night. In the morning, a bowl of watery coffee and a soggy, sticky roll, with which I felt a certain affinity. At half-past nine a crimson-faced Signora Leandri shouted:

'Come and look! The Yangtse Kiang!'

At the sound of that dream-laden name, everybody rushed to the window and stared in silence. Was it this yellowish, muddy sea that bore that mysterious, exotic name which had always stirred my imagination, and which with those other magical names like Popocatepetl, Corfu, Valparaiso and so on, had earned me high marks in geography?

I stubbornly tried to find a reflection, a tree in the water, anything which would lend a little charm or excitement to the sight of this vast slimy expanse we were crossing. Goodbye to another little dream!

Loudspeakers were filling the huge, echoing station at Nanking with the thoughts of Chairman Mao and anti-imperialist slogans. After introductions to our local guides, smiles and greetings, we walked four by four towards yet another coach. I was joined by the charming Madame Fayet who had given us such a friendly reception in Peking. She had failed to obtain permission to accompany us to Loyang and Sian. When she tried to get into our coach, the local interpreter, a pimply sourpuss, rudely waved her away.

Seeing her walk towards one of the countless cycle-rickshaws which thronged the approaches to the station, I protested energetically and informed the local guide through Shin that I insisted on Madame Fayet travelling with us, otherwise we should all get out. And I pulled the poor woman forcibly into the coach.

We were told as if it were a special treat that we were going to stay eight miles outside the town, at the foot of the Crimson Mountain.

The capital of Kiangsi province, the sometime capital of the whole of China, and the former headquarters of Chiang Kai-shek, Nanking is now a large industrial city. The old part of the city struck me as very like Sian, with the same crowded, narrow streets, tiny houses and colourful stalls. But the centre was very different, with large squares, five-storeyed apartment buildings and wide avenues. There were a great many blue and white buses, all packed with people, and with more passengers hanging on outside. The cycle-rickshaws were all occupied and at the traffic lights serried ranks of bicycles were waiting like competitors in the Tour de France.

The nearer we got to the Crimson Mountain, the cooler the air became, and soon spicy perfumes and the exquisite scents of eucalyptus and orange-blossom reached us from a harmonious park studded with silvery ponds. A concert of crickets reminded me of Provence and a wave of foolish nostalgia swept over me. Admittedly I was in very poor shape. In the course of our twenty-six hours of proximity, I had been visited by Laure's and Colette's germs.

The Crimson Mountain Hotel turned out to be a huge three-storeyed edifice in the style of the Thirties, built for Russian technicians and their families. Since the latter's sudden departure in 1960, it had been used to accommodate tourists. Big rooms, a pretty garden, a vast dining-room, excellent service. The traditional conference was held over the traditional cup of green tea. The director of the local tourist service was about forty years old and spoke perfect English, or rather American. He was likeable, gay and frank. I was dying to ask him where he had been to college in the States, but as we were not alone, I didn't dare. He immediately agreed to my suggestion—for I knew my pilgrims—that we should cancel a proposed visit to a chemical fertilizer factory. This was in fact rather a pity, because the fertilizer industry is really one of the most important in China. In any case I had no need to wrap up my request in the usual compliments and phrases, for he understood at once and was hugely amused. What a relief it was to be on the same intellectual wavelength as someone else! We were so pleased with each other that we laughed at our jokes almost behind the others' backs, like a couple of conspiratorial schoolchildren.

Jean Pariet, for his part, had ceased to make any attempt to help in working out the programme, leaving me the entire responsibility. As for the pimply little guide, seeing how well I was getting on with his boss, he put on a peeved expression. His French, I might add, was absolutely incomprehensible.

Boilèle and Signora Negri complained about the food—'only fit for savages' according to one, and 'utterly poisonous' according to the other. I preferred not to hear. On the other hand I was delighted to see that my dear Laure and Colette were visibly perking up. The general state of health of the party was improving, and I thanked heaven for the mild, dry air of the Crimson Mountain. Adrienne, though, moaned that she hadn't slept a wink 'because of that little Chinese girl in my compartment'. Shu told me what had really happened with a discreet smile: Madame Mandois had snored all night long like an old bear. But in the face of this continual whining I could feel my good will and my sense of humour, like my only skirt, wearing thin. I was finding it more and more difficult to keep my temper, and I had to make an effort to avoid snapping people's heads off and to conceal my exasperation, which got to the point where it was aroused by stupid remarks even before they were uttered.

The Chinese, on the contrary, were hardly any trouble at all. I was now quite accustomed to the slow rhythm of discussion, the high-sounding compliments and fancy phrases which were the normal means of expression, the absolute importance of never giving open expression to the slightest disagreement, and the essential habit of putting on an indelible smile and controlling one's tone of voice, whatever the circumstances. I found it stimulating to note that every day I was improving my ability to converse with them, possibly because every day I understood and appreciated them more. Their propaganda and their stereotyped opinions irritated me, of course, but that was all part of the game. And I reflected that China, alas, was not the only country in the world whose propaganda made you wince.

In the afternoon, breathing in the scented air, we walked up the long 'Alley of the Mings' where warriors and animals, twice as large as life, looked out at us from the undergrowth: a refreshing, charming walk which made me feel lighthearted and gay.

Walking through the park, I could still hear the crickets and smell the scents of Provence. Laughing happily, we finally reached a huge and rather impressive construction in white stone: the tomb of Sun Yat-sen. It was built by a Frenchman, but our Chinese escort made no mention of the fact—whether on purpose or simply out of ignorance it was impossible to tell. The mausoleum reminded me of the Victor Emmanuel monument in Rome: a horrible piece of confectionery.

Shin and Isabella climbed the steps leading up to the mausoleum side by side, chatting together. Shin kept blushing and smiling shyly. Isabella was trying the 'camaraderie' routine on him—a rather coquettish camaraderie—and it seemed to be working. Shin struck me as being won over by the camaraderie and troubled by the coquetry, although he remained very much on the defensive. Isabella looked delightful, with her peaches-and-cream complexion and her long hair. I mischievously drew attention to her slightly slanting eyes and asked Shin:

'Don't you think Isabella looks Chinese, Shin?'

'Not a bit of it,' he replied in a panic. But he took the opportunity to give her another long stare, doubtless to confirm his opinion.

The afternoon drifted by, lazy and golden. Staying in the shade and refreshed by scented breezes, I finally reached the temple of Lin-Kau, looking rather haggard and feeling a little unsteady on my legs. The temple is a massive grey stone building covered with a roof of dark grey round tiles, with a second roof half-way up. The doors have slightly lobed arches—probably a sign of Persian influence. The roof is supported by stone consoles, as in India, and the crest of the roof is lined with Buddhist stupas. The general effect is massive, sober and beautiful. This was the only monument I saw in China showing signs of a marked foreign influence.

Darkness fell swiftly. It began to feel chilly. Odette was

coughing. Laure had stayed behind in the coach. Boilèle was grumbling, Adrienne moaning. My little party seemed petrified, so to speak, in its familiar attitudes. I felt as tired as if I were fighting in a guerrilla war, with the Chinese germs wearing down the defences of my wonderful expensive American vitamins.

I had scarcely entered the foyer of the hotel when I heard Boilèle's shrill complaints drowning Shu's hesitant voice:

'It's a scandal! I've never heard such nonsense. What do you mean, I can't have a taxi? ... Madame Modiano, will you please insist on them getting me a taxi!'

I saw Shu's sullen face, and playing the part of the ham in the sandwich once again, I asked:

'Where do you want to go?'

'I want to do the antique shops,' barked Boilèle.

I turned to Shu.

'Dear Mademoiselle Shu,' I said, 'I think that General de Boilèle wants to visit your splendid antique shops. Do you think you might do me the favour of finding a car for him?'

A radiant Shu, smiling suddenly and pulling her hands out of her pockets, replied:

'Of course, Madame Modiano. You shall have one straight away.'

Confabulation with the comrade porter. Shu, being several rungs higher up in the hierarchy of workers, the comrade porter complied with her request, and a pale green Peugeot 404 drove up to collect Madame Trollan and General de Boilèle, for the greater peace of mind of the comrade-courier-for-de-luxe-tours-for-unrepentant-capitalists.

This incident confirmed my suspicions that my Chinese colleagues had decided to do everything they could to make my task easier and protect me from the wrath of my pilgrims. When a local agent balked at one of my requests, I nearly always saw Yuan's eyes harden and heard him plead my cause. Nine times out of ten, in the course of the traditional little conference which followed our arrival in a new town, I won my way—which led me to think that my trio, if not completely devoted to me, were at least loyal. Why, I asked myself, this solidarity? Was it due to my irresistible charm and torrid human warmth? I decided that it was rather because in their eyes I was a hard-working proletarian like themselves, or worse still, I was a proletarian oppressed and exploited by capitalist employers. It was a little remark of Shin's after one of Boilèle's explosions which had put me on the right track.

'It is interesting for me,' Shin had murmured, 'to see how capitalism still exploits the proletariat in the West, poor Madame Modiano.'

The two of us were strolling up and down the station platform at Anyang. I stopped, appalled, touched, and rather irritated, and looked at Shin standing beside me in a patch of sunshine. I could see in his brown eyes enormous sympathy, but a purely abstract sympathy. He felt sorry for the proletarian being exploited by a capitalist, but not for Colette Modiano being shouted at by a boor. He was indignant at what he took to be a class conflict, but which in fact was simply a display of bad temper on the part of an ill-bred individual.

I recovered from my surprise quickly enough to realize how I could turn this situation to my advantage throughout the rest of the tour. The loss of my suitcase was actually going to help me. Trailing around for a month in the same suit, which eventually began to look like a uniform, helped to integrate me with that proletarian community of the 'monoclads' to which all four of us belonged, my Chinese friends and I.


A ray of sunshine and a scented breeze invaded my bedroom, which had a large window overlooking a walled garden planted with pale green trees and brightly coloured flowers. It was half past seven. My throat felt as if it were on fire and my legs were like rubber. In the bathroom mirror I had the white face of a clown with the red eyes of an albino rabbit. Temperature: 101°. I started toying with the idea of taking the day off and leaving my companions to Pariet's tender mercies. The day's programme consisted of a visit to an agricultural commune and a fan factory. I badly wanted to visit a commune, but the idea of seeing and hearing *them* all day long was simply unbearable. Still, losing a whole day in China ... an offence against the human spirit ... To hell with that: I was an ordinary woman, and what is more, a sick woman. I was entitled to look after myself, wasn't I? I'd take the opportunity to set my hair and give myself a manicure ... No, I wasn't an ordinary woman. I was a courier in charge of twenty souls, or whatever my pilgrims had in lieu of souls! Come now, I had to make up my mind! All right, in view of the fact that there were only four or five of them who would really be interested in the problems and achievements of an agricultural commune, and considering that Pariet was an expert on the subject, I banged on the wall to call him. I put on my very best 'Lady of the Camellias' act. A hacking cough tore at my chest, and it was just a hoarse whisper of a voice that emerged from my poor body. Dear Pariet was completely taken in by my little act and expressed alarm and anxiety. I reassured him and entrusted the party to his care, with a whole series of futile recommendations: 'Don't let Boilèle monopolize you. Don't let them hang around too much—it makes them tired. Keep an eye on Laure. Explain the principle of the commune to the Blums and the Adjoufs. Don't neglect the Chapeaus just because they're shy. There's no problem with the Musketeers. Prod the others a bit and cut short the stupid questions. Try to get a discussion going with the Chinese.'

An infernal din suddenly shook the whole corridor. The dining-room was next to my room, and the shouts of the waiters as well as the noise of crockery travelled all the way along the corridor in a cascade of echoes. I tottered as far as the door and said: 'Nikao: Good day,' to the first waiter who went by. He stared at me in surprise, and I asked him in English for my breakfast. Total failure, followed by immediate recourse to picture language: a drawing of a coffee pot with steam escaping from the lid to suggest heat. I added drawings of apples, rolls, and a pot of jam. The man went off, looking as pleased as Punch, and came back three minutes later, shaking with laughter, and carrying a superb breakfast tray. I repeated my performance of the late lamented Lady of the Camellias for his benefit, adding a grimace which left him in no doubt as to my condition. He beamed with amusement and from then on looked in every hour to bring me tea, then apples, then more tea, then lunch, then a flower. About six o'clock in the afternoon he came and introduced to me his comrade successor, who said: 'Nikao,' and brought me a banana, tea, dinner, and finally his best wishes for a good night's sleep. His pal must have told him that I was the nearest thing to the Chinese concept of a funny lady. Every time he looked in, he started chuckling as soon as he opened the door. What wonderful kindness he showed me! The same kindness I met with almost every time I had a fairly continuous or repeated contact with the Chinese, together with genuine humour and above all a desire to laugh and joke, if only in gesture.

How comfortable I felt, tucked up in bed! I swallowed my remorse together with a fairly good coffee and a massive dose of antibiotics. Then I started reading an account of the Taiping rebellion, the starting-point of the history of modern China, written by a contemporary. I fell asleep and woke up again. I felt good. The bed was flooded with sunshine. I put some cream on my face and hands. That was delicious. I went back to sleep. The same noise of shouting as in the morning woke me up. Lunch. I got up, washed my hair with a special quick-drying lotion, set it, and treated myself to a manicure and a pedicure. The day was beginning to drag a little. I felt worried: was everything going all right? I only hoped Noiret hadn't made any sarcastic remarks about the inadequate mechanisation of Chinese agriculture. I fell asleep again. The window banged, the sun had disappeared, large blue shadows lay across the garden. A knock at the door. My 'little darlings', accompanied by Madame Fayet, came in to feel my pulse and tell me all the news. They were followed by the Three Musketeers, Pariet, the Italians, the Blums, the Chapeaus and the Adjoufs. They all sat on the bed and the floor and started laughing and joking. Georges Wolf presented me with an old painting on silk he had just bought, and Alexandre Dupont with a hand-painted fan. They looked pleased to see me and said they had missed me. I was touched. Admittedly I was feeling feverish, and at time like that, everyone feels an added need for affection. Even Adrienne appeared and posed theatrically in the doorway. I felt happy and reassured to see them all there, and all in high spirits. My lovely stolen day was over.

# 17

An old piece of flannel on a bag of nuts: that was what I felt
like next morning, sitting in the train. For the first time we
had some Chinese passengers sharing our compartment. From
their gabardine clothes I concluded that we were in a *de luxe*
carriage. The seats were arranged in pairs, facing each other
across a central corridor. Between each pair was a table covered
with an immaculate embroidered cloth, and on each table stood
a vase of chrysanthemums. I sat down with Dupont, Noiret and
Shin. I started laughing helplessly, followed by my neighbours,
at the sight of our tired little group jolting about like the heroes
of the old Hollywood Westerns in which the travellers in a
stage-coach are shaken up and down to suggest the speed of
the vehicle and the bumps in the road. Our seats, designed for
little Chinese bottoms, were extremely narrow, and we sat rigid
and erect like bishops in a medieval council. Madame Chapeau
nodded off. General de Boilèle, bouncing up and down like an
old tennis ball, kept bumping his chin on his chest. In her
hieratic silence Adrienne for once was almost impressive.
Laure's blue eyes met mine across the corridor and lit up with a
mischievous gleam. Georges kept sneezing. In spite of the heat,
he was wrapped up in a medley of cashmere shawls, skilfully
graded from beige to moss green. The others were reading or
chatting. The Italian women were playing gin rummy, but
Isabella was bored and kept darting sidelong glances at Shin.

Shin for his part was explaining to Laure and Colette that
China had nine political parties, which all enjoyed propor-
tional representation in the National Consultative Assembly.
Our scepticism—a benevolent scepticism on account of our liking
for Shin—could be measured by the depth of our silence. Shin
went on imperturbably:

'The widow of President Sun Yat-sen is Vice-President of the Consultative Assembly.'

'I seem to remember, my dear Shin,' I broke in, 'that she is the sister of Chiang Kai-shek's wife, and that both women are the daughters of a rich banker called Song.'

'That is correct,' Shin retorted curtly, 'but Sun Yat-sen's widow immediately joined the ranks of the people and has never ceased to live in accordance with the thoughts of our beloved Chairman Mao.'

Dupont asked quietly:

'What would happen if Chiang Kai-shek came back to China? Would he be executed?'

At this question Shin got up abruptly and went to consult Yuan who was asleep with his mouth open a few seats away. After a while he came back and said:

'If Chiang Kai-shek returned, he would be well received and due honour would be paid him. If Chairman Mao considered his autocriticism to be honest, there would be nothing to prevent him from receiving an official appointment suited to his abilities, such as membership of the Consultative Assembly.'

This reply left us open-mouthed with amazement. Oh, wise and admirable China!

Noiret's face turned red—a sign of aggressiveness in him—and he asked:

'Is the Kuomintang represented in the Consultative Assembly?'

'Of course,' replied Shin.

'How many members does the Kuomintang have in China today?'

Though embarrassed, Shin replied firmly:

'I don't know.'

'Why do you know the number of members of the Communist Party,' asked Noiret, 'and not of the other parties?'

'Because,' came the answer, 'on the anniversary of the foundation of the Communist Party, Chairman Mao announced that the Party had seventeen million members.'

A pretty Chinese pirouette!

'Shin,' Noiret continued, 'do you know the date of the anniversary of the foundation of the Kuomintang?'

My bag of nuts turned into a pincushion. Noiret's unpleasantness struck me as unfair to Shin, who did everything he could for us in the friendliest way. I managed to change the subject by going into ecstasies over the scenery which had become tropical since we had left Nanking. Fields of maize stretched away to the horizon, and buffaloes waded through the silky green paddy-fields, drawing wooden ploughs. Both men and women wore huge round flat straw hats which served as little portable parasols. It was becoming very hot in the carriage, and the shrill music coming over the loudspeaker was giving me a headache. I asked Shin to switch it off. He went and asked permission to do so from each of the dozen Chinese passengers at the other end of the carriage. Each in turn agreed, and I thanked them one by one with a smile or a nod of the head. The musical caterwauling stopped, as did the piping feminine voice which had been singing the usual praises of ... Guess Who.

# 18

At last a station which looked like the Gare Saint-Lazare, almost as old-fashioned and almost as dirty. At last people running and pushing without looking where they were going. For some reason, here in Shanghai, I no longer felt I was at the far end of the world. My flock chatted and stretched lazily in the moist midday heat. But what was this? No red carpet? No flowers? Just a bust of Chairman Mao? Could the South of China be as easy-going as the South of France? We would have to see.

In the reception hall a little speech of welcome; on our side, a little speech of thanks. Rooms were allocated to us, and then promptly reallocated by me while we were driving through the district of the old French concession. Crowded streets, one or two-storey houses, windows with little panes of glass. A great many bicycles, shops huddled together, their displays spilling out into the roadway. Children squatted in the gutter, calmly opening their breeches, which had a large slit in them for that express purpose. The classic blue overalls of the Chinese worker had been mended so often here that they looked like American patchwork quilts. The men's clothes were all rather dirty. That was something new. Their faces were more haggard, their eyes sadder. On the other hand the women, who had previously looked like convicts and walked like all-in wrestlers, here wore trousers which fitted their figures closely. Their white or floral blouses were clean, and they almost looked chic. They smiled and looked at the men. Shu, with her hands in her pockets, her basin-crop haircut, and her baggy trousers, looked like a yellow quince, was conscious of the fact, scowled angrily, and almost ignored their remarks and their smiles. She admitted to me that this was her first visit to the South and that she regarded people in the South as neither very serious nor very respectable. I had heard that sort of comment before. 'Dear friends in the South of every country,' I said to myself with a sigh, 'whatever you do, never become serious and respectable!' At the idea that a tiny particle of frivolity had managed to stand up to the steam-roller of the Revolution, I felt reassured, as if everything had finally returned to normal, comforted by this touch of humanity in a Spartan setting.

Here I was not in China any more. This was a Chicago which hadn't had a single lick of paint since 1925. We had just driven into the Bund, the Wall Street and Fifth Avenue of the Concessions, the former avenue of the banks, the leading import-export firms, and the big hotels. I discovered with astonishment the dilapidated ghosts of early twentieth-century capitalism. On the left, greyish office blocks; on the right, the torn, copper-coloured sail of a junk belonging to the eternal China.

The contrast reached its peak when I entered the heart of all the pomp and luxury of yesterday's China, the holy of holies, once reserved exclusively for whites, the famous Peace Hotel, formerly known as the Sassoon Hotel. Crossing the worn carpets of the vast 1900 foyer, I reached the porter, who spoke neither English nor French. My room had the look of a down-at-heel Ritz. The chandelier was by Gallé, and threads were showing in the velvet of the armchair. The enamel of the bathtub was streaked with yellow. It was shabby luxury, but luxury all the same. In the dining-room the table linen was dazzling white, the silver English, the waiters dressed in livery. Most of them were old, very distinguished, and spoke English. The generation of transition.

After lunch, an army of weasel-faced and vaguely hostile interpreters took us up to the roof-terrace of a skyscraper which before becoming a hotel was a brothel for American troops from 1945 to 1949. After the Americans had left, the building was occupied by the families of Russian technicians. It stands at the junction of the Whangpoo and the Soochow river. We could see the whole river below us. In the distance, the black mushrooms rising from the factory chimneys were melting into the grey mist. Junks with their yellow sails spread were cleaving the muddy waters of the Whangpoo, which wound like a long snake alongside the grey office blocks. Motor boats were carrying people and goods. At our feet was an unexpected sight: the British Consul's residence, with the Union Jack flying above it, and a lawn and flowerbeds around it. Set among their trees and magnolias, many former European residences had been turned into schools, offices and institutes. It was easy to imagine the opulence which had once reigned here, side by side with utter destitution. The opulence had disappeared, and the destitution was now only poverty. Traces of melancholy rose from that shameful past, mingling with the grey austerity of the present.

On the right, the two-storey houses built by the Europeans, the brick warehouses and the factories reminded me of the dirty, shabby London of the dockland districts by the Thames.

This hybrid city, not really Chinese but not in the least Western any more, gave me a feeling of malaise. Standing on that hotel roof, I reflected sadly that the West had brought nothing to Shanghai but poverty and suffering, and in the end had left nothing behind but a few ugly buildings which were ageing badly.

As we were driving once more through the former French concession, our weasel-faced, twitching interpreter suddenly spewed up a torrent of venom about the atrocities committed by the French during the colonial era. What he said was probably true, but scarcely tactful. Protesting to his superior later on, I obtained an apology, and the interpreter perhaps received a reprimand. For the moment he was taking the 'loathsome French' to an antique shop which turned out to be the Galeries Lafayette of antiquity, with one department for enamels, another for ivories, a third for porcelain. We were dazzled, overwhelmed. Seized by a spending lust, the 'capitalists' poured their yuans unstintingly into the coffers of the People's China.

I tried to have a chat with the antique dealer, a charming old man who spoke perfect French and English.

*C.M.:* 'Do you own this shop of yours?'

*The Dealer:* 'I have a share in it.'

*C.M.:* 'How big a share?'

He lowered his eyes and pretended he had to speak to one of his employees. In any case before the Revolution he might also have lowered his eyes without replying, for the Chinese hate personal questions. How I sympathized with them! But as the possibility of spending every weekend in China was denied to the greater part of suffering humanity, I silently begged their forgiveness and resolved to be rude. Returning to the attack as would the late lamented fly, I asked the antique dealer if he had occasion to meet many tourists.

'Oh, yes!' he replied with a smile. 'More and more every year, I'm pleased to say.'

Those I had brought into his shop, like a cloud of locusts, were methodically buying up everything, in serried ranks, department by department. Nearly everything was modern, but the imitations were excellent. Here and there, lost in the mass, there was an antique jewel, or a few mandarin buttons in jade. I tried to imagine the fate of their original owners: a melancholy exercise. The antique dealer stopped trying to avoid my questions. He even seemed pleased to rediscover the scent of a past which must have been much more pleasant for him than the present.

'The fact is,' I said mischievously, 'that you're a capitalist of the new régime!'

'To a certain extent that is true,' he replied with a smile. 'In any case I have an enviable situation. I am very fortunate.'

The reply was rather vague, but I had discovered that in China people talk a great deal through silences. My thick Western hearing was beginning to get used to Chinese conversation. At least the antique dealer, for one, hadn't talked to me about the thoughts of Chairman Mao, or about the revolutionary achievements of his government.

I continued my interrogation:

'How was your life before the Liberation compared with the life you lead now?'

I had gone too far. The only answer I received was a frozen smile. And the next moment the antique dealer had disappeared behind another counter.

Marquis Torti bought a pretty antique jewel for his beautiful friend Signora Coli. Colette completed the collection of snuff-boxes she had begun in Peking. But the champion of the shopping expedition was little Madame Neralinda. While her Peruvian banker husband sat huddled on a chair, waiting obediently, vague-eyed and flabby-lipped, she rolled like a little ball between the counters, picking up, putting down, clicking her fingers, nodding her head, waving gaily to her husband, and then continuing her zigzag course, followed by a flood of white packets accumulating behind her. It was a rather horrifying sight, in spite of Madame Neralinda's smiling charm and real niceness of character. It was as if she were afraid that something might escape her, and I reflected that this urge to possess everything that came within reach must spring from a terrible inner hunger. Standing in a corner of the shop, Shu was sulking.

'I think it's revolting,' she told me, 'the amount of money these capitalists pay to buy useless trinkets of the past.'

'Come now, Shu,' I said, 'calm down. These trinkets may be useless for them, but not for you Chinese.'

Shu suddenly turned aggressive.

'What do you mean?' she asked.

'I mean, Shu, that your economists have very cleverly enabled your foreign "friends" to acquire your knick-knacks of the past. That provides them with a nice supply of foreign currency which allows you Chinese to buy from abroad the machine tools, tractors and raw materials you lack. Even if you regard her as ridiculous, you should bless Madame Neralinda and her like, who after all are unconsciously behaving as friends of China.'

Shin hadn't missed a single word of my little lecture and looked absolutely bewitched. Shu, on the other hand, was obviously hostile, and clearly thought I was brainwashing her. Each of them was as utterly ignorant as the other, despite the fact that both were students. They lived in a completely closed world, and received only a very fragmentary, dogmatic education. It was this rather than any indoctrination which made conversation with them so difficult. We were always talking to them about things or questions of which they did not so much as suspect the existence. This used to infuriate Pariet, who never emerged from his abstract world of Western intellectual socialism. He was alternately mad with rage and in the depths of despair when he saw that these marvellous Chinese intellectuals at whose feet he had expected to sit like a little child knew nothing and understood nothing, least of all his own thoughts which he expounded to them with generous abandon.

During my course of political economics, my charges had been buying frantically and putting my theories into practice. I felt a little tired. After astonishment came satiety. I had the same sort of vague headache as the pastrycook's boy who has eaten too many chocolate eclairs.

And then, all of a sudden, we were whisked off to the 'Exhibition of the Industrial Achievements of the People's China'. This exhibition was installed in a horrible palace with thick grey columns erected to the glory of Sino-Soviet friend-ship, and the entrance was adorned with two Russian and Chinese giants holding hands in a stone grip which it had been impossible to loosen after the break of 1960. Walking through the endless marble-paved halls, I noted a dentist's chair, a machine for counting blood corpuscles, a few transistors, and a cheap imitation of the Simca 1000 which fascinated our Chinese companions.

'You haven't got a car like that in France?' Shin whispered to me. It was not so much a question as a statement. Propaganda and obscurantism. Walking slowly beside him, I told him that I had a car, and that the same was true of many French people, even among the proletariat. I trod very cautiously, taking care not to describe a traffic jam in the rush hour. I badly wanted him to believe me, because I knew that he trusted me. I did not want to arouse a chauvinistic reaction in him, nor to offend him, nor to make him think I was blowing some capitalist trumpet.

Our conversation was interrupted several times by Boilèle, who kept shouting:

'Shanghai's a terrible bore—it's all modern. The programme has been bungled: we're staying here too long. Madame, change the timetable and let's leave earlier.'

Adrienne was groaning that she was tired and her feet were hurting her. Georges Wolf was a little depressed and looked sad. Alexandre Dupont was propping up Laure, who was trotting about, smiling all the time, and insisting on seeing everything. Faced with a model of a refinery, she and I agreed that there was something pathetic and admirable about this frenzied effort to survive the Russians' desertion and isolation from the world. These men who had emerged from nothing, and who were keep-ing their heads above water at the cost of an enormous effort, were utterly fascinating, and the curiosity they aroused in me, far from being satisfied, was growing all the time. But the farther we had penetrated into the heart of the country, the more I had begun to realize that I understood and knew nothing about China. There, perhaps, like some of my companions, I had taken the first step, possibly the most difficult step of all. I had promptly thrown overboard all my preconceived ideas, preju-dices, superficial judgments, hasty deductions. Yet although I knew nothing, I still felt some emotion and even a sort of tenderness for these little men and women who apparently knew nothing either—nothing, that is, but the essential fact of life: that every day you must struggle to survive.

I slipped out by myself at nightfall, through the side door of the hotel, which opened on to a street running at right-angles to the Bund. It was a fairly wide avenue lined with big shops whose lighted windows displayed bicycles, footballs, one-piece bathing suits for women, pans and dishes in aluminium, and radio sets in wooden cases. There was no sign of anything in plastic. I forked off to the left. Suddenly the scene changed. The tall street lamps disappeared. Along both sides of the narrow street were rows of soup kitchens with a dense crowd pressing around them. Each soup-dealer was perched on a little stool and kept plunging a ladle into a big cauldron wreathed in clouds of steam. One by one they filled little bowls in floral porcelain which they held out to their customers. For 5 fens (2d.) I obtained a bowl myself. The soup was excellent and tasted of fish. I then plunged into the crowd as it moved silently along. The faces I saw were tense and thin, some even haggard. The people looked sad, or rather as if their thoughts were far away. My presence aroused neither curiosity nor hostility: nobody even saw me.

Soon I came to a sort of flea-market for old clothes. On both sides of the street, stalls made of old canvas, sheets of corrugated iron and pieces of cardboard were held together with bits of string and wire. Rails ran from one end to the other of each stall, offering a selection of blue cloth trousers, shirts, pullovers in thick coarse wool, and gabardine jackets. There were a few quilted jackets, traces of the passage of inhabitants of some remote region, Manchuria perhaps. Everything was poor and shabby, but clean and never evil-smelling.

Night had fallen. The shops along the big avenue were still lighted and still empty. I suddenly realized that I was being followed. The man stopped at the door of the hotel when I went inside.

# 9

The museum took our breath away. A mass of rare pieces heaped up, piled high, crowded together. Chou bronzes, Han and T'ang pottery, and Ming vases in profusion. When I asked the local guide where these treasures had come from, he replied grudgingly:

'The former capitalists voluntarily presented us with their collections.'

Not particularly convinced of the 'voluntary' nature of these gifts, I also felt sorry that nobody told us anything of the progress and discoveries made by Chinese archaeology, which had presumably made some contribution since 1950 to the formation of this remarkable collection.

All these treasures were contained in a succession of showcases which were opaque with dust. There was no identification apart from a few labels which even Shin was incapable of deciphering, and which Pariet scorned to examine, reminding me that 'this wasn't his province'. Torti went into ecstasies over a showcase containing a score of Chou vases, superb bronzes as big as cathedral bells.

'Shin,' I said enthusiastically, 'what a magnificent museum!'

'You really think so, Madame Modiano?'

And looking rather embarrassed, Shin admitted that he knew nothing about the art of the past.

'You mean it doesn't interest you?'

'No, not in the least. It isn't important and it distracts us from our principal aim.'

Knowing perfectly well what he was going to say, I asked perfidiously:

'And what is your aim, Shin?'

'The fulfilment of the thoughts of Chairman Mao.'

So much for you, little T'ang dancers, crushed for all eternity beneath the weighty thoughts of the Prophet. I noticed two or three little men in their forties, wearing caps—presumably workers—and farther on, a group of children walking along in silence, and I asked Shin:

'Those people over there seem to be taking an interest in the futilities of the past. Who are they? Dangerous reactionary revisionists like us?'

Shin swung round abruptly, saw that I was smiling at him, relaxed, and finally smiled too.

'Madame Modiano, you are terrible. It's impossible to talk seriously to you, you joke all the time.'

Unfortunately for me, he didn't.

Between the museum and lunch, after my charges had dispersed, either to the antique shops or to the Friendship Shop, the local department store, I slipped out of a side door for another walk by myself, this time beside the Whangpoo. Strolling beside a river is the best way I know of getting to know the kaleidoscopic features of an unknown town. For it is by the river that people come to idle away their time and abandon themselves to their emotion of the moment, whether it be love, sadness, gaiety or meditation. The air was warm and moist. Facing the Whangpoo there was a boy with his arm round the neck of a girl in pigtails. This was the first time since I had arrived in China that I had seen a couple displaying their affection in public. Some men in clean blue trousers and white shirts walked past. They looked tired and gave me hostile stares. Again this was the first time this had happened to me. A little farther on, four girl students carrying books under their arms openly laughed at me as they went by. I carried on exploring, though I was beginning to feel a little ill at ease. A bent-backed man with hollow, ashen features looked at me with real hatred and spat noisily in my direction. Luckily he missed me, but mentally I felt sullied. As I was crossing the Bund on my way back to the hotel, a skeletal old man stopped his cycle-rickshaw in front of me and with a tired gesture invited me to get in. None of these things had happened to me before. Life here definitely seemed to wear a different face. It was clear that the system had not established so complete a grip on the South as on the North, and that individuals had not been so radically transformed. Once again, the appearance of the women offered a good idea of the economic condition and the political atmosphere of the city. Here the women were not dressed in blue overalls. Their floral blouses and smiling faces seemed to suggest a certain remoteness from the great melting-pot of the Revolution.

I returned to the hotel along the pavement in front of the former banks and office buildings, reflecting that this hatred I had seen for the whites was simply the sorry result of decades of contemptuous racialist colonialism and the economic looting in which the Western nations had indulged in a spirit of joyful competition.

In the afternoon we installed ourselves in groups of three in a line of long black cars of Soviet manufacture. It was raining. I had wet feet and a heavy heart. Our programme consisted of a new district and an old district. After and before. This sounded like a piece of cake...

The cars drove along a long avenue lined with little hovels which were not even equipped with chimneys. On the pavement in front of each house a tiny cast-iron brazier served as a cooker and heater. The cars stopped at a crossroads, where a woman with the serious, unlined face of a nun came to shake hands with me and assure me that our visit represented a great honour for her district. For it was she who was in control of that particular section of Shanghai, and her district was called Tien-Chau. As she led me along the main street, which the rain had turned into a quagmire, she told me that before the Liberation this area had been a mosquito-infested swamp whose wretched inhabitants were decimated by epidemics. She showed us a mud hut similar to those we had seen earlier beside the big avenue. It was in this sort of hovel, she explained, that the inhabitants of her district used to live. Now these huts were disappearing one by one and the local council was rehousing the families in new districts.

An old woman greeted us with a smile on the threshold of her poor dwelling. A bicycle was propped against one wall. A little radio in brown bakelite occupied a place of honour on a piece of deal furniture which was presumably used for the cult of ancestors. There was no running water. All around were similar hovels, some thatched, others covered with broken-down tile roofs. The floors were of beaten earth. It was a typical shantytown scene, but without any shanty-town smells. Everything was clean and tidy and well swept. The inhabitants themselves wore patched but clean overalls and black felt slippers.

We made a brief stop in a sort of reception hall, a long whitewashed room which served as a library, studio and cultural centre. A television set in one corner of the room was protected by a cardboard box. The walls were covered with garish posters showing Negroes, Chinese and Arabs shaking their fists in admirable unison at some invisible enemy. Punctuating her monotonous tirades with a jab of her right forefinger, our guide informed us that we were now on the site of the former crematorium of the district.

In spite of the slowness of the translation and the inevitable praises of Chairman Mao which studded our hostess's speech, my pilgrims seemed to be fascinated by this encounter with a precise, visible social situation. Only Boilèle and Adrienne kept shifting in their seats and grumbling. I asked our hostess:

'Who lives in Tien-Chau?'

Touched by the interest we were showing in her problems, she replied that many of the local inhabitants had come from less favoured districts. Worker Sun Yen-sion, for example, who lived in Lodging No. 7 in the 4th Subdivision, used to share an area of twelve square yards with six members of his family. The rain used to leak into his hut. Now he occupied an area of nineteen square yards and enjoyed the use of sanitary equipment. Carpenter Chou Mei-tsung, who occupied Lodging No. 10 in the 4th Subdivision, lived here with his wife and four children. He was now earning £20 a month and had been able to buy a radio (£7), a bicycle (£20), and even a watch (£10). Before the Liberation, he and his family had had barely enough to live on, and had had no money for clothes. They had been able to buy themselves clothes and furniture. Their monthly rent was between 4d. and 6d. a square yard for the living-room. Water and electricity cost them between 8d. and 1s. per person per month.

I had a lump in my throat and I was not the only one. This simple exposé, translated into staccato phrases and giving only basic facts, was a thousand times more moving and convincing in its stark simplicity than any Maoist parable. It was obvious, and we all knew it, that people used to die in the streets in thousands in China, as they still do today in India. Whether we like it or not, in Mao's China nobody dies of hunger any more. True, overeating is not a problem likely to affect the country in the near future. The Chinese will remain a lean people for a long time to come, but they seem to be assured of the basic minimum.

I looked closely at this woman with the serene, waxen face while she told us the story of a third worker. The dogmatic character of her faith annoyed me slightly, but I was getting used to that, and I reflected that this woman who probably had no material possessions and whose only reason for living was the hardest and noblest task in the world—ensuring first the survival and then the livelihood of a few of her compatriots—was worthy of admiration and envy. Feeling tears come into my eyes, I told myself that I really must be getting tired, and also that our Western form of democracy was a luxury which only well-fed peoples could allow themselves.

The right forefinger went on wagging like a metronome.

'Since the Liberation,' our hostess told us, 'even human nature has changed in China. People have become honest. This year, in our district alone, two thousand pieces of lost property have been returned to their owners. What is more, everybody here helps his neighbour, ignoring his own interests. True, the present standard of living is still very low, but it is much higher than it used to be. In any case, the people are aware that they are building up the country under the leadership of Chairman Mao Tse-tung and the Communist Party in whom they have placed their entire trust.'

It was impossible to avoid the traditional tirade. But this time it was worth hearing.

Now it was time for the questions of the honoured visitors. This was the moment when I usually felt rather ashamed.

'Have you got a cultural centre?' asked Adrienne, suddenly waking up.

'This is it,' replied our guide. 'We put on performances organized by local amateurs: plays, songs, poetry competitions, and also television and cinema shows.'

I suspected Adrienne of having heard the expression 'cultural centre' somewhere and of having tossed it off with only the vaguest idea of what it meant.

'What does the sanitary equipment consist of?' asked Colette Quesnel.

'Each lodging,' came the reply, 'has its own equipment, which includes a W.C. but not a bath. There are several families on every floor, and therefore several sets of equipment.'

'What proportion of the population,' asked Claude Adjouf, 'is made up of children?'

'About fifty per cent.'

'That's enough talk,' said Adrienne. 'Let's see for ourselves.'

Walking along a muddy yellow path we came to a single-storey building which was the dining-hall for the old people of the district. The retiring age for women, we were told, was fifty, and sixty for men. About thirty men and women were playing cards, sitting in groups of four round wooden tables. They stood up as we came in, smiling and clapping. Some of them looked old and worn out, but several struck me as quite hale and hearty, and still capable of doing a job of work.

I asked if they had any occupation, the younger ones at least. Did they look after children, for instance, as sometimes happened in the North?

'No,' our guide replied proudly. 'For them, retirement means a rest after a working life which has often been very hard.'

As soon as we arrived anywhere, a claque of children and young teenagers sprang into action. It broke into a storm of joyful applause as soon as the head of the column of tourists appeared. I paid our guide a series of lengthy compliments. At a signal from a man standing in the background, the crowd drew back to allow our cars to move away. Then a bunch of children clustered round us and pressed their noses against the car windows, staring at us with eager curiosity and responding warmly to our goodbye waves.

As we drove past a four-storeyed concrete apartment building, unoccupied as yet but with its balconies already yellow with damp, I learned that there were ten million people in Shanghai to be housed and that the government had so far been able to rehouse only a million.

Back in Paris, people had talked to me in lyrical terms about the Children's Palace in Shanghai.

'You'll see,' they had said, 'the children are the triumph of Red China. Chinese children are absolutely adorable.'

In fact, we discovered that there were twelve children's palaces in Shanghai. The one we visited had formerly been a wealthy merchant's residence. With its staircase of polished wood, its dark panelling and its multicoloured floor-tiles, it looked very like a luxurious Paris town-house built about 1900. Massed in the doorway, twenty children rushed at us, grabbed each one of us by the hand, recited a little compliment in a loud voice and relentlessly dragged us after them. It was out of the question to let go of the sweaty little paw which was holding my hand like a vice.

We went through a succession of rooms full of children drawing, or playing cards, chess or spillikins. The best drawings, all in a very academic style, had been pinned on the walls. In one room we interrupted a concert of Chinese music; the flautist was very charming. In the scale-model room, fighter aircraft were dangling from the ceiling. Next came the military training room, where a boy was learning how to handle a sub-machine gun, and a little girl of seven was crawling under a barbed-wire entanglement fitted with little bells—without touching them, needless to say.

'This is to ensure our defence in the event of attack,' the guide told me through the weasel-faced interpreter, who was keeping a watchful eye on me.

I gave a sudden start. Screeches were coming from the next room. It was Signora Negri shrieking:

'It's disgraceful training children for war! By teaching them your aggressive attitudes you'll start something horrible, and God will surely punish you.'

'Be quiet, Mama,' whispered Isabella, shaking her mother by the arm. The poor woman was completely hysterical and went on shouting and talking about God and religion. Pushing everybody aside, I went over to her, and with Isabella's help dragged her into the table-tennis room. Table tennis is of course the national sport of China, and Shin, impassive but still pink with emotion, reminded us that the world champion was a Chinese. In the huge glass-walled room the sound of the balls was like machine gun fire. Adjouf, who decided to show off his skill, was pulverized by a little girl of twelve who slowed down at a discreet signal from Shin. Suddenly Shu sidled up to me like a little shadow and whispered:

'You are wanted on the telephone from Paris, and so is Madame Quesnel. We must go back to the hotel straight away, because the telephone connections are cut off at six o'clock, twenty minutes from now. There's a car waiting outside.'

I left the group in Pariet's care and rushed after Shu, at the same time paying silent tribute to an organization which made it possible to find an individual in a city of ten million inhabitants. Admittedly the number of tourists was very small, and it was known where they were at any given moment.

In less than a quarter of an hour we reached the hotel at the other side of the city. I dashed along the corridor, beating Colette by a short head, dived into my room and snatched up the receiver.

'This is Madame Modiano. You have a call for me from Paris. Hurry please.'

'Here is Paris for you, Madame,' said a Chinese voice.

And there indeed was Paris, a Paris which came to me in alternate waves of sound and silence. I had to fill in the blanks for myself. It was wonderful, that voice from the other end of the world speaking to me in such a familiar language. It warmed my heart. I came out of my room radiant with joy, to find Colette utterly disconsolate. Beaten to the post, she had been forced to wait for the end of my call before she could have hers. There was only one line, they had told her, and now the connections had been cut off. The poor thing! Her disappointment really upset me. But I felt not the slightest twinge of remorse!

# 20

During dinner I went from table to table taking names for the various tours planned for the following day. The Musketeers and the Adjoufs were going to see a people's commune with Laure, under Pariet's guidance, while the Chapeaus and the Blums wanted to visit a factory. Boilèle waved me away and decided to take the Italian ladies round the antique shops. So much the better! He was really becoming a pain in the neck. Signora Leandri and Colette Quesnel wanted to go to the University with me. Adrienne hesitated. University or antique shops? University, antique shops? Univ-antiq? Uni-ant? My heart was pounding wildly: there was no doubt about it, my nerves were beginning to feel the strain. Damn: she had chosen the University. 'Good night, sleep well.' I snuggled down happily in my soft bed after putting away my solitary suit with infinite precautions. Hanging all by itself in the luxurious dressing-room with the mahogany drawers, the poor thing was beginning to look like a dented old mussel.

After a dreamless night and breakfast in bed, which confirmed once again the fact that I appreciate luxury as much as I can do without it, I met my team-mates, who were in excellent spirits. Colette was as elegant and charming as ever. Signora Leandri was kindly and jovial. Adrienne arrived simpering sweetly, her face looking all the more painted in that such artifices seemed incongruous in China.

The Dean of the University, a woman of about thirty-five with a gentle, intelligent face, was waiting for us in front of one of the long pink brick buildings which housed the University, and which were surrounded by trees and lawns. Tea was served in the usual drawing-room furnished with leather armchairs and a bust of Mao. The Principal, a man in his forties, with an intellectual face, gold-rimmed spectacles and a blue tunic buttoned up to the eyebrows, recited his little 'before and after' speech in a rather embarrassed monotone. In the midst of all the usual nonsense in praise of Chairman Mao, we picked up a few interesting pieces of information:

'Forty-five per cent of the students now come from working-class families, whereas before the Liberation all the students at the University belonged to the bourgeoisie. Forty per cent of the students come from families in the liberal professions, and only fifteen per cent come from the former bourgeoisie.'

At Shanghai University, we were told, each student could choose his faculty, which was not the case at other universities, where it was the student who was chosen according to his marks, his abilities and his health, notably in the science faculties.

I asked the comrade principal if, in the Faculty of Political Science, for example, the students took much interest in international politics.

'Both professors and students,' replied the Principal, 'take an interest in world affairs in order to raise their "level of awareness". They study the works of Chairman Mao and Marxism-Leninism.'

'Do they have any vacations?' asked Colette Quesnel.

'Yes, five weeks every semester, which they spend in a factory or an agricultural commune. And every five years the professors devote an uninterrupted period of two months to manual labour.'

'Why?' asked Colette.

'Because, unfortunately, of the continuing influence of the corrupt old bourgeois society. There remain in fact many signs of a contempt for manual labour and an erroneous belief in the superiority of intellectual work. That is why the Government imposes manual labour on all intellectuals. After spending some time in a paddy-field or a textile mill, the intellectuals lose their class arrogance and feel greater understanding for the manual workers. That is why the foremost members of the Government and even our beloved Chairman Mao have taken part in building our dams and laying down our railways.'

The Principal repeated this last sentence three times, looking morose and irritated. Or perhaps it was our interpreter who knew only a single speech in French and kept on repeating it untiringly? How were we to know? Neither Shin nor Shu was present, and the local interpreter had great difficulty in expressing himself. We were treated to superficial 'before and after' comments on every laboratory, every building, every department of the University. Leaning further and further back on his sofa, the Principal recited his litanies with increasingly obvious boredom. I waited for the moment when he would ask us to point out his deficiencies and favour him with our criticism. As a token of friendship, of course. My toes started curling in my shoes at the prospect. Another cup of greenish tea. It was a toothless old man in black slippers who filled my teapot with boiling water. He was very well trained, and must have been in the service of the Rector of the 'contemptible University' which existed before the Revolution.

I felt angry with the pompous idiot of a Principal for my own irritation. For it was true that in the old days only the children of the well-to-do could go to the University, and that that University was indeed 'contemptible', since the rich Chinese preferred to send their sons to Europe or America. The new régime's achievements spoke for themselves, and trying to prove too much with the same everlasting arguments only wearied the most sympathetic and open-minded onlookers. The Principal continued:

'All the subjects which didn't exist before—biology, biochemistry, biophysics—are taught here today.'

'Even nuclear physics?' asked Colette.

'No, not yet,' growled the Principal.

I in my turn asked how much time was devoted to research and whether research students were free to choose their field of study. In reply I obtained a confused explanation that research students were 'free to choose the subject of their research in conformity with the requirements of the State'. We learned that all the professors lived at the University with their families, paying a rent equivalent to four per cent of their salary; that all the students were lodged free of charge; and that seventy per cent of them—the proportion of the student population that came from poor families—were given free board as well. About a third of the students were girls, and it was in the Biology Faculty that the greatest number of girls was to be found. Each student had about twenty hours of lectures every week, in the mornings, and twenty-eight hours of private study.

All of a sudden a shrill bell rang out. It was ten past eleven, and the end of the morning's lectures. The students crossed the lawn, walking in rows of four, like a long blue ribbon. Our little group followed them, looking very incongruous in that world of blue uniformity.

'I want to see a French class and an English class,' Adrienne kept insisting, with an exquisite delicacy matched only by Colette's exasperation and my own.

On the pediment of the Modern Languages School we could read some mottoes in English: 'Develop yourself morally, physically, and intellectually,' and 'Be cultured workers with socialist minds.'

With Signora Leandri following us like a fat seal dragging her flippers, we took our places on the benches of a language laboratory. Each desk was equipped with headphones which relayed a text in English, French, German and Russian. The French voice, distinguished, rather affected, very Comédie-française in fact, recited a passage from Karl Marx about the achievements of the working class which was extremely rich in vocabulary. Instead of a blackboard there was a screen on which we were shown a film with a commentary in English on the increase in steel and petroleum production and the construction of a chemical fertilizer factory.

The next room was a sort of radio studio. Adrienne pounced on the microphone, and before we realized what was happening, recited a little society speech in which she spoke of her joy in being there and the happiness she wished all her listeners. These pearls of rhetoric were broadcast by loudspeakers to the four corners of the University. Colette and I writhed in shame and embarrassment, but the Chinese never batted an eyelid. The absence of any sign of emotion in other people is sometimes very comforting.

In the students' library, a large, well-lighted room which looked out on some trees, and which was furnished with wooden chairs and tables and lined with Chinese books, we found an official translating a beautiful piece of calligraphy. The text was a saying of Mao: 'Flames can set fire to a plain.' On a wooden hoarding there was the familiar poster showing a Negro, a Chinese and an Arab brandishing their fists. At the top of the poster were these words in English: 'Freedom now.'

In another corner of the room another hoarding carried a display of photographs taken in Cuba and Czechoslovakia. One of them showed some Filipinos waving a banner which said: 'C.I.A. Public Enemy No. 1.' In another photograph some Indonesians were painting 'U.S. go home' on the walls, while a third showed two American officers standing by the debris of their plane after it had been shot down over Vietnam. It reminded me how poignant pictures of prisoners always are.

Outside, students were still walking past in rows, giving the impression that it was the same group which was going round the block and, like actors at the Opera, coming back on to the stage.

Our next visit was to a dormitory. We went into a white-painted room containing eight bunk beds standing four by four against the wall. In the middle of the room was a large table and eight chairs, and on the wall a huge photograph of Mao and two calligraphed posters. A couple of paper roses were standing in a vase on a shelf. The students' blankets were folded in squares at the foot of the beds. In response to the stupid question I asked him—'Do you work hard?'—a bespectacled young man with prominent teeth replied politely:

'Oh, yes, we work hard for the future of the Revolution which has brought us happiness.'

His English was correct, his accent reasonably good. At these words, his fellow students who were massed in the corridor smiled and clapped. Good Red Guard material.

We took leave of the Principal, who had not abandoned his morose expression for a single moment. Was he violently hostile to foreigners? Or was he secretly opposed to the régime? Or was he simply suffering from an ulcer? Or all three? The frustrating thing about this kind of encounter was that one would never know.

As we were leaving, the friendly woman dean who had met us on our arrival translated for our benefit a few passages of a typewritten text posted up on a big hoarding. This was the autocriticism of a student who accused himself of having misunderstood Mao's order reducing the political and academic activities of all students by a third. He confessed that he had rejoiced unduly over this order, simply out of laziness. But now he realized that this brilliant edict issued by the revered Chairman was indispensable for the preservation of the physical and mental health of the students. There followed a long list of the wise instructions laid down by our hero.

'Ignoramuses! Utter ignoramuses!' hissed Adrienne, who was probably under the impression that Karl was one of the Marx brothers ...

To occupy the afternoon, for which nothing had been planned, Yuan suggested that we should go and see a 'repentant capitalist'.

We drove through the industrial districts in the Northern part of the city, along wet, narrow streets lined with leprous grey walls, with occasional gaps which revealed grubby huts and muddy yards where inky water was oozing from pyramids of coal. Perched on these black hills, men and women with only a piece of oilcloth to protect them from the rain were filling tall round baskets which they then loaded on to carts.

Chatting with the new interpreter who was accompanying us, I told him of the admiration and emotion I felt at the effort being made by the Chinese people. Shin, who was with us, translated what I had said for Yuan, who turned round and spoke to me, gazing at me intensely as if I could understand Chinese. Shin told me that Yuan was suggesting that I should stay at Peking University and teach French there. I guessed that this flattering proposal had not sprung spontaneously from Yuan's brain. It presumably reflected a decision taken by the relevant authorities. I explained that I had a daughter who was still very young, but that in a few years I would be happy to return, and that in any case it would be an honour for me to make my small contribution to the immense edifice that was China. Saying this, I noticed that I was becoming increasingly Chinese in the expression of my ideas. I was even beginning to give little nods of the head while I was talking to people.

A water main had obviously burst, for the street we were driving along was flooded and the car passed between two sprays of black water. I ventured a joke, saying:

'Chairman Mao doesn't need to go as far as the Yangtse Kiang for a swim!'

I promptly regretted my weak effort at Western humour. But Shin translated what I had said. Roars of laughter came from Yuan and the Shanghai interpreter, who seemed to be hugely amused. Yuan asked if I could swim. I replied that I could, but that he mustn't worry: Chairman Mao could soon put half the

F

width of the Yangtse Kiang between us. More laughter, punctuated with hoots of merriment.

In a yard which was bigger and cleaner than those we had glimpsed on our way, a middle-aged man in a smart beige raincoat greeted us warmly, though with a hint of embarrassment. Holding me by the elbow (he was the first Chinese to touch me in any way except a handshake), he led me through a cotton mill employing six thousand workers which he used to own and which he now managed for the State. He did not give me a single technical explanation but strode through the workshops as if he were on a grouse-moor. I was amused to see the obvious disappointment of my companions as they trailed sadly behind me. They had come to see the survivor of a defunct régime, a piece of human detritus left alive by the new régime he hated and feared, and here they were, galloping behind a portly, well-dressed gentleman who was actually ogling that survivor from the hard-labour camp of capitalist society, their own courier!

At the end of the marathon through the mill, the manager, without consulting the interpreter, pushed me into his private car. I must be dreaming, I thought. But no, it was a gleaming black Jaguar, and a very recent model at that—last year's, my host told me. The Shanghai interpreter got in after us and sat down on the front seat. I began a conversation in English, a language which our host, Mr. Wong Jong-yi, spoke fluently, having spent two years in Birmingham as a trainee in a mill. He answered my questions readily enough, and told me that in 1949, at the outbreak of the Revolution, he had fled to Hong Kong with his wife and three children. He had dreaded the arrival of the Communists, who not only stripped all the bourgeois of their possessions, but also, so it was said, practised 'common ownership of women'. All the same, the following year he had gone back to China 'to see for himself'. Presumably provided with solid guarantees, he had returned to Hong Kong to fetch his wife, and his children had followed the next year. He told me that he still went to spend a couple of weeks every year in Hong Kong where some of his relatives were still living. He explained to me that 'workers and capitalists have joined together here to increase production', and that since 1955 his mill had been a joint enterprise of which he remained the manager. He spoke to me about the terrible poverty of the Chinese

154

cotton workers after the war, at the time of the Kuomintang. China was then importing ninety per cent of her cotton from the United States, and this had practically ruined the local industry. The Chinese mills had ceased to serve as anything but finishing shops for the American mills. The smaller work-shops had had to close down, and the same process, repeated in other spheres, had resulted in complete economic dependence. He had considered at the time, like a few other liberal industrial-ists, that China could only become and remain a nation by gaining her economic freedom. That was why he had freely decided to co-operate with the Communist Party, which was the only party pursuing that aim.

He seemed to be very much at ease. Was he being sincere, or was he caught in a trap and forced to keep up a pretence? Both, perhaps, depending on the circumstances. After about ten minutes the interpreter suddenly said a few words in Chinese to Mr. Wong Jong-yi, who immediately turned to me and said in his excellent English:

'I must apologize to you for my inadequate command of English. It would be better if I spoke in Chinese and your in-terpreter translated what I said.'

His embarrassment reappeared, his eyes clouded over: the current had been switched off. The interpreter, of course, spoke no English. To save the manager's face, I asked him a few harmless questions in French. He promptly launched into a violent attack on Western propaganda which was forever criti-cizing China. I assured him that he had no idea how much sympathy and curiosity China aroused in Western Europe, how many articles were published on the subject, and how disastrous and blameworthy the Western liberals considered the economic and political isolation in which part of the world tried to keep his country. I didn't mention the name of America, for in China more than anywhere else, you have to know 'how far is going too far', and America, for the Chinese, is 'too far'.

Our conversation, commonplace in subject and more leisurely in tone, continued as far as his home. This was a pretty house full of carpets, fine lacquered furniture, chandeliers, and show-cases crammed with T'sing porcelain. The comrade-owner-man-ager's wife was dressed in a flannel skirt and a cashmere sweater. She gave us tea served by two maids in white aprons. We started asking questions, but our host cut them short and in a shrill voice recited a little speech summing up our conversation in the car. He was no longer the same man; now he was awkward and nervous. We formed a circle round him in the big ground-floor drawing-room. Then the two maids, dressed in black jackets and trousers and white aprons, served us with little cakes. The lady of the house, completely absorbed in her duties as a hostess, fussed over us in the Chinese manner, with a humble smile belied by the despotic flash of her eyes.

As for the master of the house, he assured us of the honour which our visit represented for him, especially as he received very few foreigners. I didn't believe a word of this, for I was convinced that the Chinese frequently showed their visitors this curious example of a marriage between capitalism and Communism. Our host, we learned, received an annual interest of 5% on his capital as valued in 1956. This interest amounted to eighty thousand yuans or £13,000 a year, which were paid into his bank. Since he was unable to spend all this money, he left a considerable proportion of it—three quarters, he told us—in his account. He could not invest any money, nor buy another business, nor acquire any more property, not even paintings and *objets d'art*. Twice already, in 1962 and 1965, this *modus vivendi* had been given official approval. His house, furniture, car, private possessions, everything the Party had left him in the way of property, could be left to his heirs without any payment of death duties. He pointed out to us that his was not an exceptional case. Shanghai numbered several hundred managers of big factories who enjoyed the same advantages, and several thousand small capitalists who had retained partial or complete ownership of their businesses. Often the interest on the capital invested in these businesses was insignificant, and the owners had chosen to receive a fixed monthly stipend instead.

What, I wonder now, will remain of this survival from the past after the Cultural Revolution? Will the capitalist Wong Jong-yi be able to continue driving his Jaguar through the howling masses of Red Guards? Before leaving him, I asked him whether, when he drove in his Jaguar past one of his workers hitched to a heavy cart, he didn't think that in the eyes of that worker he represented the very image of man's exploitation of man.

'Of course I do!' replied Mr. Wong. 'But that worker knows as well as I do that exploitation is a contradiction of society, an abnormality, and is therefore doomed to disappear. He also knows that his life is going to improve and that exploitation cannot last because the capitalists have agreed to give their property to the people. So the difference between capitalists and workers can only diminish. And that's the main thing.'

The incredulity and irony which greeted these words were so tangible you could have cut them with a knife. My companions were outraged by these niceties of handing over property, taking it back, losing it, returning it and renting it. They didn't know what to make of it. And everything about this affair which might seem to confirm the common sense and moderation of the Communists was completely inconsistent with their idea of 'what things were like in Communist countries', and reduced them to sniggering bewilderment.

With countless precautions and excuses Colette Quesnel said to our host:

'Forgive me for being so indiscreet, but your case has an extra interest for us in that it might be ours one day. Has your life changed a great deal?'

Mr. Wong shook his head.

'There is no difference,' he replied, 'between my material circumstances now and before the Revolution. I have kept my house and my servants. It's my way of life which has changed. I've done with the gambling, the wasteful spending, the sophisticated life of the past. That's why my expenditure has gone down so much.'

'What do your children do?' asked Laure.

'My eldest daughter,' he said, 'is a student in the Faculty of Medicine in Shanghai. She's a member of the League of Youth. My second son is studying physics at the College of Science and Technology. My two youngest children are at secondary school. None of my children wants to be a capitalist. All of them are perfectly integrated in the new society and well adjusted to their new way of life.'

I noticed a certain sadness in this man who tried to appear so jovial with his perpetual smile. The material side of his life was one thing—you could believe what he said or not, but in any case he was doing very well for himself. But it was different with his children. I got the impression that it hurt him to see that his children were strangers, creatures of a different species who no longer thought like him and did not want the same things as him. His voice had changed. Madame Wong, with her smiles and compliments, never batted an eyelid, and with her grey clothes reminded me of a little blade of tempered steel.

The musical-comedy maids relieved us of our teacups and served coffee.

Our host returned to his subject, volunteering the information that old-age pensioners received sixty per cent of their salaries after ten years' service and seventy per cent after fifteen, and that small capitalists received a high rate of interest. What was more, he explained, children were now educated by the State, and material problems had disappeared. As for the small minority of capitalists who didn't work, they were suitably indemnified.

In spite of these fine words, the effect he created was increasingly depressing. He had spoken all the time in Chinese, which was translated by the interpreter. You got the impression of a compulsory performance. This middle-aged man, probably a liberal to begin with and certainly a favoured citizen now, could obviously not be expected to express any sort of nostalgia. All the same, the contrast between the enthusiasm of his words and the sadness of his expression upset us all. We could sense that he was afraid of our questions, that he felt embarrassed. I decided to cut short his ordeal. He and his wife courteously accompanied us to our cars. Laure and Colette lingered behind for a moment to thank them effusively. Our host seemed touched, his wife delighted.

In the car Yuan tried to pump me, asking me for any criticisms I might like to make. This invitation always made me feel uncomfortable and once again I said nothing. I caught sight of a boy with his arm round a girl's shoulders: a rare sight, like a smile in all this drabness. At the hotel there was a heated argument, much of it irrelevant, among my charges.

'It isn't his house,' Signora Negri stated flatly.

'The car is a compulsory gift from the Party to impress visitors,' declared Torti.

'Poor fellow, having to play the fool for a lot of foreigners!' sighed Madame Chapeau.

Laure and Colette sent flowers to Madame Wong. This kindness didn't surprise me, coming from them. They were the only ones to show it.

After an excellent dinner, admirably served, still divided into two groups of 'Chinese eaters' and 'European eaters', we found

158

ourselves back in the coach. It was with our heads buzzing with racy reminiscences that we set off to spend the evening at the *Grand Monde*, the former giant brothel. A horrible grey, ugly, five-storeyed building arranged round a yard and fitted with balconies outside. On the ground floor, a gallery of distorting mirrors; on the upper floors, paved with asphalt, crowded auditoriums in which people were laughing and listening in fascination to edifying plays, clowns and storytellers. A host of stalls selling fritters, pies, sesame loaves and noodles. A maze of rooms hung with drawings showing superstitions which ought to be abolished. A silent, well-behaved, happy crowd, nibbling food and indifferent to our presence. Within half an hour we had seen everything. I herded my flock back into the coach, leaving behind only the Musketeers and Pariet, all four of them probably a prey to some vague nostalgia. An impression of poverty and weariness followed me into the wet, deserted street. We returned to the hotel in silence, shivering slightly.

On the train to Hangchow the next morning, Pariet told me that he had left the Musketeers at the *Grand Monde* a quarter of an hour after our departure, to come back to the hotel by himself. After going a few yards he was accosted by a shadow which emerged from a wall, a man who politely offered in Chinese to take him back to the hotel, for fear he lost his way. Pariet replied in Chinese, thanking him for his offer but declining it. In vain. The shadow insisted on its anxiety at the idea of a foreign friend getting lost. All of a sudden Pariet felt himself literally lifted off the ground and hurled on to a passing tram. The shadow helped him off the tram when it reached the hotel and only let go of him, with a courteous farewell, outside the door, where it remained standing until Pariet had disappeared from sight. The poor fellow was quite put out by the whole affair, and I couldn't help laughing. That was wrong of me, because he was stumbling from one disappointment to another, and his humanitarian liberalism was suffering from every incident on the journey and every word spoken by the Chinese, with whom he argued bitterly for hours, using French left-wing arguments which struck them as so much gibberish. He was really quite touching, and so naïve that I felt as if I were his grandmother ...

# 21

We arrived at Hangchow at the beginning of the afternoon. The skies were grey. We drove along the shores of a lake which was sad and silvery. Some mountains stood out in gentle silhouette in the distance. The hotel overlooked the lake and the gardens around it. There was a slight commotion among my companions because not all the rooms had a view of the lake. I allotted those which did have a view of the lake to the married couples and the women on their own, while I lodged the men in the rooms facing the forest. I installed Madame Trollan in one overlooking the lake and her friend Boilèle in another which was very close but which looked out on the forest. Alas! A storm of Latin anger broke out, with a violence which formed a painful contrast with the surrounding half-tones. I quietly begged the Chinese to try to get me a few more rooms overlooking the lake, stressing that they would be doing me a great service. I could feel them weakening. At that moment Noiret rushed up to us, as red as a turkey-cock, and snarled:

'You keep asking us for criticisms ... well, I'm going to give you one now! Allow me to inform you that in France travellers are all treated the same way!'

I broke out in an icy sweat. Shin, all pink-faced, turned round slowly and said:

'Do you mean to tell me, Monsieur Noiret, that there are no rooms at the back of French hotels?'

Boilèle then burst out of Madame Trollan's room with a view, grabbed me by the shoulders, and started shaking me.

'You always treat me worse than the others. I shall complain to your director. You wait and see what happens to you when you get back. In any case I've had more than enough of this filthy country!'

The faces of the Chinese went blank. It would have been funny if I hadn't felt so ashamed. I released myself from Boilèle's grip and sent everybody off to lunch, including the Chinese.

Colette Quesnel, with typical sweetness, solved my problem for me. She gave up her room overlooking the lake, which I gave to Boilèle, installing Noiret in the General's old room, from which you got an oblique glimpse of that damned piece of water. I then moved Georges, whose window looked on to a heap of coal, into Noiret's room. Choking back tears of rage, and dragging my suitcases along the corridor myself, I for my part moved into the coal-hole and finally collapsed on my bed for a few moments, to ease my aching back and try to regain some semblance of serenity.

The 'Chinese eaters' stood up as I came into the dining-room, embraced me, fussed over me, and forced me to have some lunch. Noiret looked embarrassed and avoided my eyes. Shin eyed me anxiously and whispered:

'I think your Monsieur Boilèle could do with a period of re-education.'

Yuan spat impassively into his handkerchief. As for Boilèle, when I handed him the key to his new room, which was really Colette's, he leaned back in his chair and said:

'You see! I told you there'd be a way!'

Total silence around the table of the 'European eaters'. He was disavowed by all his neighbours, who came over to tell me so, one by one. I tried to imagine the impression all this had made on the Chinese, who already considered us selfish and devoid of community spirit when we were at our best.

When we met again at three o'clock the atmosphere was still strained, the more so as it was now pouring with rain. Our coach drove alongside the lake, which was shining like a sheet of mercury in the fog, to Hangchow itself, a town of six hundred thousand inhabitants. It was a rather sad, dull place, with the only picturesque touch provided by a street of covered stalls selling combs, scissors, sweets, soap and ivories.

We dragged our wet feet into a brocade factory, where we saw nothing but some rather ugly artificial silks, and notably some silk panels a yard wide depicting Marx, Engels and Mao.

On our return to the hotel we felt as if we were bathing in liquid mud. To ease my nerves I went for a walk in the beautiful park planted with pine-trees. This solitary walk in the rain was sad but refreshing. The earth smelt good. The turned-up roofs of the houses glistened in the rain, men and women passed me in silence, and night fell over Hangchow, which an ancient proverb likens to a paradise on earth.

Hangchow was in fact a famous spa frequented by well-to-do Chinese before the Revolution. The villas built in the 1900 European style on the hills round the lake had been turned into old people's homes, sanatoriums and nursing-homes by the new régime. I thought to myself that, new régime or not, a spa in the rain always gives an impression of boredom and stagnation.

By the following morning the rain had stopped. The lake, the surrounding hills and the dense vegetation were all wreathed in a silvery mist. The scene had the tranquil, leaden greyness of the tropics. As soon as we left the town, we found ourselves driving between flowerbeds, shrubs of different varieties, and coral-trees. The road wound across wooded hills whose slopes were cut into terraces. These terraces were planted with tea-shrubs: round bushes studded with small white flowers. The harvest was over, but two girls mimed the gestures of tea-picking for our cameras. The village, or rather the commune, was very pretty, with whitewashed brick houses covered with double roofs of grey tiles. We were served with 'Dragon's Well' tea, the most famous tea in China, we were told, in an attractive room with handsome dark wainscoting, where we sat around a massive dark wood table. Our hostess was the director of the commune, a lively little woman of about forty who had been re-elected every year since 1952. She told us that the commune received sixty per cent of the price obtained from the sale of its tea, of which it kept twenty francs for the purchase and maintenance of its equipment. She also informed us that there are thirty thousand leaves in each pound of tea, and that the best tea is that which is picked during the first ten days of the first harvest. However, she did not know the price at which the commune sold its tea to the State.

'That probably depends on the quality,' was all she said in reply.

She proudly showed us all over the commune. which was extremely clean. Healthy-looking children were running about the paths. Women dressed in blue and carrying baskets hopped from one step to another, smiling at us. The school shone like a new pin. The walls of the two classrooms were covered with multicoloured posters inviting the children to cut their nails, wash their clothes and do exercises 'to prepare themselves for the defence of the country', advocating 'work and discipline' and declaring that 'Lenin is the great protector of the people'.

Leaving the group to its photographs, I went out of the village and plunged into a bamboo forest. The slim golden stems rose to a height of several dozen feet, crowded together and letting through rays of sunshine like dazzling arrows. The air was sweetly scented. In front of me, in the powdered sunlight, a shadow approached: it was a peasant carrying a couple of buckets hanging from the ends of a bamboo pole balanced on one shoulder. I looked into the buckets. They contained pig manure, which, together with seven per cent of their land, belongs to the peasants. He was furious at being photographed and hid behind a tree. Animal manure has always been one of the greatest riches of China, and also one of its greatest sources of shame. Under the *ancien régime* hundreds of families made small fortunes by buying 'human manure' street by street and district by district. In those days the servants of every house used to leave it in a little hut at the end of the street. Those huts have now disappeared, but human excrement is still collected in both town and country in big wooden buckets with heavy lids.

Shin told me later that the government was giving considerable attention to the building of new chemical fertilizer factories and the development of those which already existed. For the moment, he said, there were very few, and the amount of chemical fertilizer which was produced was still extremely small in relation to the needs of Chinese agriculture. Manure accordingly remains the brown gold of China . . .

Farther on, I saw two girls washing clothes in the stream which wound along beside the path, and then, amazingly enough in prudish China, a boy bathing naked.

In the afternoon the sun gilded the lake, which had been dredged to make it possible to go boating on it. We embarked four by four in boats on which green tea was served under a canvas awning. Standing in the stern, a woman pushed on a long oar. The shore receded into the distance, and with it the luxurious holiday homes converted into sanatoriums, the pine plantations and the bamboo forests. Feeling very languid, I disembarked on an island ablaze with chrysanthemums. I crossed some little arched bridges, walked beside tiny pools which shone like mirrors, crept through the undergrowth, revelled in the scent of countless flowering shrubs, and finally reached the 'Bridge for Contemplating Goldfish', where, like everybody else, and just like visitors to the Carp Pond at the Château de Fontainebleau, I threw bread to the fish.

Laure tore me away from my party and the goldfish to tell me that Shin and Yuan had installed themselves in her boat and Colette's, and had surreptitiously handed them pamphlets advertising tours organized by Luxingsche, the Chinese travel agency, explaining that if they wished to return to China it would be in their interest to apply to him, Yuan, because like that their journey would cost much less than the tour they were on at the moment. This was a strange thing to do. I wondered whether it was inspired by a desire to sabotage a capitalist organization, or to an obsessive longing to fight the profit motive, a motive considered immoral in China.


On the way back, watching Hangchow appear, all red and black in the setting sun, I thought about the passion for drawing comparisons which takes hold of us all at the sight of a new landscape. For a writer such as Simone de Beauvoir, Hangchow is the Athens of China; for a Dominican priest called Father Lelong it recalls Capri.

For all that it had been the capital of the Sung emperors, it did not strike me as a place where the spirit blows, not even the spirit of pleasure, but simply an ordinary Chinese landscape. But what did that matter? We had all had a pleasant and refreshing outing in the country, all the more refreshing in that Boilèle was in bed in his room—his room overlooking the lake —with a severe attack of colic! Poor Noiret—for whom I felt some sympathy—was suffering the same agonies. I met him wandering miserably beside the lake, looking rather green about the gills. I took his arm and the two of us returned to the hotel, chatting together. He was upset too because the Musketeers hadn't been speaking to him since his outburst of temper the day before, and I promised to put in a good word for him. It was really rather funny, I decided, this impression of being a schoolmistress in charge of twenty more or less impossible brats.

The evening was spent at the Opera, where a Chinese Communist resistance fighter had a bone to pick with the Kuomintang and the Japanese. The audience, which consisted mainly of peasants, was very poorly dressed. The people's faces struck me as more tired and emaciated than in the North. One after another we all fell fast asleep. At the interval I took half my flock back to the hotel, explaining that they were suffering from the ravages of Asian flu. During dinner, at which the service was not as good as it had been elsewhere, Laure made a tremendous scene because the tablecloth was wet. Our waiter was petrified. Without any visible sign of spite he brought us a jelly made of lotus roots. Ugh!

The next day, standing in a pool of sunshine on the steps of the hotel, I found an individual with a waxen complexion. It was Boilèle. Oddly enough, I was pleased to see him, I had been so afraid of having to trail a moribund general around with us. In spite of his weakness he summoned up the strength to point a furious finger at a delegation of French-speaking Negroes embarking on the gleaming lake.

'Look at that!' he roared. 'Even niggers are treated better than we are. *They* get motor-boats!'

Soon troubles started crowding in on me. Shin informed me that on our flight to Canton the following day we would be entitled to only fifty pounds of luggage per person. Our excess luggage would be sent on after us by train: in other words it would arrive in Canton after we had left China for Hong Kong. I let out a loud oath which embraced in a single malediction ill-bred reactionaries, stupid regulations, and even the golden lake which had caused me so much trouble.

I then issued an announcement asking for all excess luggage to be left in the corridor the next morning before my flock went to Mass—for I had had to find them a Mass in the heart of Red China!

I looked for Pariet to entrust the group to him. He had gone off for a walk by himself, abandoning all interest in the party. When he got back I outlined the day's programme for him in a voice which I couldn't prevent from being curt, and set off with Shu for the airport. I could find nobody there. At the check-in desk there was only a pathetic individual, a new-style coolie who knew nothing and understood nothing. On every table in the reception hall there were pamphlets in Chinese and English about the thoughts of Chairman Mao and the war in Vietnam, written by the Australian journalist Wilfrid Burchett.

On my return to the hotel I tried to soothe my nerves by looking at the scenery. In front of me lay an immense market garden planted with vegetables in squares about a hundred yards across, so that it looked like a green and yellow patch-work quilt. The peasants lived in wooden huts covered with tiles or thatch. Everything looked very clean and tidy. When I opened the window to breathe in the country air, I was hit in the face by a strong smell of manure. There were people working in the fields in groups of about a dozen. Some were resting. The air was warm and humid. The boats on the pretty little streams looked as if they had been placed on pieces of mirror-glass. Behind the houses I caught sight of the big wooden buckets intended for the collection of 'human manure'.

I went out to sit on a bench by the lake and write a few letters. Every child who went by came and stood behind me. Soon there were a score of them laughing at my pen as it ran across the paper from left to right. They rocked with laughter, holding their sides and even weeping with merriment, but without making fun of me. What I was doing just struck them as terribly funny.

In the afternoon Boilèle was sick again. The evil side of my character got the upper hand: I was delighted. But we began getting our pagodas and emperors mixed up, especially as neither Pariet nor our Chinese guides illuminated our afternoon's sight-seeing with their brilliant explanations.

At one point Signora Leandri maliciously whispered to me:
'Adrienne and the General are trying to train the Chinese! But they'll never do it! Today when the servant brought Adrienne her tea, she told him: "Will you kindly take your hands out of your pockets!"'

Pariet had announced that in the evening he would be giving a lecture on the Sung dynasty. This was to be the last lecture of a series which had often been extremely interesting. Shin asked me on Yuan's behalf for permission for the three of them to attend it. I had previously taken care never to hold any lectures in the public rooms of a hotel, but always in one of our own rooms, to avoid the risk of being accused of expressing subversive opinions in public. This time, at Yuan's suggestion, we installed ourselves in one of the hotel drawing-rooms, and I decided to take the opportunity to give a small party. I ordered some little cakes and a sherry-type wine.

Pariet opened the flood-gates. Shin, sitting just behind Yuan, provided him with a simultaneous translation. At the end of the lecture, while I was passing round the cakes in a merry din, Yuan asked if he might say a few words. I asked everyone to sit down and listen. Yuan explained that he approved of the facts given by Pariet, whose standard of education he admired, but that he disapproved of the interpretation placed on those facts. There was a stunned silence. Then Noiret exploded in a shrill little voice:

'Then let's hear his own interpretation! That's all we're waiting for!'

'What a nerve!' yelped Adrienne. 'So he disapproves of the facts, does he? The very idea!'

Poor, woebegone Pariet had never had so many supporters. Yuan smiled, his eyes gleaming. After a confabulation between Shin and Yuan, Shin explained his colleague's viewpoint in somewhat confused terms:

'In the entire history of the world, it is always the people who have done everything—sharing out land, conquering countries, producing works of art—and not generals or so-called emperors.'

And that was that! The criticism was a little brief, and offered a curious contrast with Pariet's intelligent lecture. Seeing that Noiret was getting ready to lead the sniggerers into battle, I hurriedly sounded the retreat.


On the morning of our departure, helped by Shin, I collected the suitcases outside the various rooms, to the accompaniment of howls of protest from Boilèle, who swore that 'nobody told him anything'. I had decided to try to send the excess luggage by air. Arriving at the airport in a bone-shaking coach filled with sixty suitcases, I found a fairly competent girl at the check-in desk, together with the coolie I had seen the day before.

We had seven hundred pounds' excess luggage. The plane, I was told, could not take it. I insisted, pointing out to the young woman that it was in the airline's interest to take the suitcases and make me pay an excess luggage charge, whereas if the suitcases went by train, no government department would receive that money. The girl looked as if she were thinking this over. My heart started pounding wildly. She plunged into some catalogues. Shu made a mysterious signal to me and time went by. I felt myself growing old. Finally the girl emerged from her calculations and spoke to Shin, who told me:

'It's agreed, but it will be very dear. That's why they never do it.'

Prepared for the worst, I asked:

'How much?'

'.45 yuans for every pound of excess luggage.'

Ninety centimes! Quick, my mental abacus! Help, my memories of school arithmetic! At last I had the answer: six hundred and thirty francs. A mere trifle! Out of a sense of decency I assumed a serious expression. The little peasant porters had come over and were looking at me as if I were a Martian. I took out of my handbag, one by one, six wads of five-yuan notes and three separate notes. The poor cashier had never seen so much money in her life and started counting the notes with a clumsy thumb. Some young people gathered round me, their eyes as big as saucers. It was with a light heart that I returned to the hotel to pick up my party and bring them to the airport, where this time I was greeted with smiles.

We boarded a Viscount with blue plastic fittings. It was gay, pleasant and very European. There were a few Chinese in gabardine suits on board and they did not seem to notice the horde of noisy whites who rapidly took over the aircraft.

The take-off struck me as rather slow—so slow, in fact, that I looked up from my book and saw to my alarm that only one propeller out of two was turning. I looked at the other wing: the same was true there. A stab of panic! I don't know very much about aeronautics, but all the same, taking off with only two engines out of four struck me as pretty daring. I only hoped my flock wouldn't see what was happening. Blum leaned towards me: he had noticed. I whispered to him to keep quiet.

Noiret had noticed too and, alas, started telling the others. Luckily by now we were well and truly airborne.

'It's to economise on fuel,' explained Shin.

I decided to economise on myself a little from then on.

# 22

Two hours later the humid, scorching air hit us in the face like a towel soaked in hot water. We waited in the torrid atmosphere of Canton airport while the local interpreters came and went, chirping and pirouetting in a little ballet. One of them informed me that we were going to spend the first night fifty miles outside Canton, for every hotel in the city was full, on account of the Fair which had attracted two thousand foreigners. I grumbled wearily. In vain. The first interpreter was then followed by a second who told me that for this night in the country we were to take only our hand luggage with us: the rest was to remain in the left luggage department. This time I got on my high horse.

'I'm willing to accept the difficulty in finding us accommodation, because I imagine you can't do anything about that, but I refuse to agree to submit my group to considerable discomfort just because you want to economise on the cost of a coach or the work of two or three porters. That is absolutely unacceptable and I find it hard to reconcile with the traditional laws of Chinese hospitality.'

Yuan kept nodding throughout Shin's translation. I felt that I was strongly supported on the left, so to speak, and I pressed my point. The Cantonese had a private consultation and gave in. I began to see what a little determination could do, and I insisted on a drive through the city before we went off to our distant refuge. The coach drew up outside a park full of shade, birdsong, flowers and perfume. A cool breath of air caressed our faces at the very entrance.

'The antique shops, the antique shops,' chorused Boilèle, Adrienne and Noiret.

'What do the majority want?' I asked.

No reply. The majority wanted nothing. Nobody wanted

anything. They had all had enough: they were finished. I said goodbye to my rustic stroll in the pretty park. Off we went to the local antique shop, which, as it happened, was a great disappointment, but which was situated beside the River of Pearls, so called on account of its milky colour. I was fascinated by the junks on the river, whose red and brown sails, often in tatters, swelled out in the warm breeze.

The city itself was very lively, but far from clean. In the colourful crowd, many of the men wore white shirts, while the girls wore light blouses, but never skirts. Once again, the people's features looked more hollow than in the North. Noiret kept digging his elbow in Dupont's ribs.

'Look at the girls, old man, they're much better-looking than they are in the North. That one over there is terrific!'

The great continence of Mao's China was obviously beginning to tell on some of my pilgrims.

The poorer districts were swarming with people. Narrow streets lined with small houses were littered with carts, cycles, stalls, and baskets on the pavements. The rooms we could see into were tiny, and full of women and children. There was no silence here, but squealing, shouting, arguing, swearing. The houses of the former residential districts looked like French seaside villas in 1930, except that here they were half-hidden by palm-trees, banana-trees and hibiscus. Nothing had been painted for twenty years, the walls were flaking, black streaks marked the façades, and washing was hanging in the windows.

Chou-Hua, the remote rural paradise where we were being housed for the night, was situated at the end of a long road which we travelled at nightfall in a jolting coach. Moist air came in through the open windows. The road was full of ruts, and on my seat at the back of the coach I bounced up and down like a ping-pong ball. Georges Wolf, who was sitting next to me, was repeatedly shaken by violent fits of coughing. Draped up to his eyebrows in a huge cashmere shawl, he was sweating profusely in his two roll-top vicuna pullovers. On the next seat Shin was smiling happily at Isabella. Behind him, Shu, sitting next to Pariet, turned her head away. I couldn't tell whether Shu had a soft spot for Shin, if indeed it is still possible for anyone to have a 'soft spot' in modern China, but it was obvious that she loathed Isabella. Pariet, for his part, had fallen out with the Chinese ever since he had lost his temper on the train from Nanking to Hangchow trying to win them over to his socialo-liberalo-democratico-Jacobin revisionism. The poor man was very bitter and found it impossible to understand why respect for human rights should be an unknown commodity in China. I had tried to explain to him that things didn't work that way in China, that both the purpose of life and the driving force behind the Chinese were different. But he was just as stubborn, and just as sincere, as my Chinese colleagues, and he refused to listen to reason. On the practical level this made things rather difficult for me. In any case it didn't create a cordial atmosphere at the back of the coach. The pimply, obsequious interpreter leaned towards me with a slobbering smile.

'What do the French think,' he asked, 'of the American atrocities in Vietnam?'

To blazes with him! Whatever I might think, I had no intention of telling this purulent monkey, and I sent him off with a flea in his ear.

'Go to France,' I said, 'if you want to find out what the French think. For the moment, what interests us is China, not the United States.'

The hotel had the same blotchy walls and damp silence as a seedy seaside boarding-house in the off-season. In my room the curtains and the mosquito-net were torn, and the water supply was cold and parsimonious, but the garden smelt of pepper and orange blossom. In the corridor, Adrienne, wigless for once, moaned:

'I want some milk and a couple of apples. Yes, that's enough for me. I'm not at all difficult. Send them up to me straight away, won't you?'

But there wasn't the ghost of a waiter anywhere. It was an absolute desert. So much the worse for Adrienne, who appeared in the restaurant repeating her apple litany, probably in the hope that some man in the group might compare her to Eve. In vain. There are times when sheer fatigue spares you a few vulgarities. We drank a sweetish, warm champagne which gave me a headache. I asked Shin, who had really become very friendly, to try to get hold of some cars, instead of the coach, for the return journey to Canton next day. Adrienne had not had her apples. For the second time Shin remarked:

'There are some people who would benefit from a period of re-education.'

The next day we woke up in paradise. We were on the shores of a lake surrounded by paddy-fields and forests. The sun was turning the landscape pink. After breakfast I went for a walk along a path lined with coral-trees and picked some orchids. Then we set off on the return journey to Canton. This time the day was beginning, instead of ending, in the meadows and the paddy-fields. The peasant women were arriving in a slow procession, wearing huge straw hats surrounded with a sort of black fringe, presumably to filter the light and keep away insects. Teams of workers, stripped to the waist, were widening the road, by digging up the banks of red earth lining it.

In the crowded, torrid centre of Canton, on the corner of two streets loud with shouting and the rattle of trams, I trickled out of the coach to find myself in front of a doorway half-closed by a corrugated shutter. This was our hotel. In a small tiled room with leprous walls two boys of twenty were chattering away behind a counter and paid no attention at all to my arrival. I called Shin and displayed a certain impatience. The two local beatniks casually handed me cards bearing the numbers of our rooms. They informed me that the married couples in our party would have rooms with twin beds, but that those who were travelling alone would have to sleep three to a room.

What! My pernickety *de luxe* tourists, already condemned to staying in a hovel, were now expected to sleep in threes! I promptly moved behind the counter, grabbing Shin by the sleeve and motioning to Shu to come back quickly. I then embarked on some tough talking to the two young jokers, who were openly making fun of me. I accused them of fraud, reminding them that our classification as luxury tourists entitled us to better accommodation. Sniggers from the two boys. Shin started getting irritable. I pointed out the folly of what they were doing:

'After such a successful tour, how stupid it would be to leave friends of China with an unpleasant memory! The last impression is always the one that counts most. It would be heartbreaking if that impression were a bad one.'

Shoulders were shrugged. Canton, I decided, was definitely Marseilles, with a touch of Corsica thrown in. On the other side of the counter I could hear Boilèle shouting:

'This is all the fault of the Paris organization. They are responsible. If something goes wrong in my bank, I'm the one who's responsible. Well, this is the same, isn't it?'

Laure tried to calm him down.

'For heaven's sake shut up. There's no comparison. When *will* you understand that we are in China, in a completely different world?'

Colette came and whispered in my ear that she and Laure would like nothing better than to share a room with me, and that the Musketeers too were willing to doss down together. I was touched, but decided, for the principle of the thing, to put up a last fight, especially as an irrepressible anger, like any anger which has been suppressed for a month, was rising to my nostrils.

'If you don't find me ten single rooms I promise you that I shall lodge a complaint against you in person with the Embassy of the Chinese People's Republic in Paris, stating that you are sabotaging the tourist industry in Southern China. I give you a quarter of an hour!'

I was foaming with rage. The picture I presented must have been terrifying, for the beatniks sprawled out behind the counter sat up and then sprang to their feet. One of them picked up the telephone and started yelping into it. Boilèle for his part was still howling. It was really rather funny, for I had started a positive panic. Shin looked very pleased. The boy who was phoning hung up. Shin grinned broadly and told me:

'You've got your ten rooms. But some German industrialists who are arriving later won't get theirs!'

I was exultant at having not only got my way but also done the Germans in the eye. Sedan, Verdun, Montoire and the rest were avenged! I silently hoped that the unknown Germans would be devoured by fleas *en masse* and not one by one. For I was sure that this damned hotel was infested with fleas. My squalid room opened on to an evil-smelling corridor through a cracked door with a fanlight over it. The bathroom floor was covered with a torn piece of old linoleum, and cockroaches were frolicking about at the bottom of a prehistoric bathtub streaked with rust. The two guards on duty on our floor were shouting at each other in the narrow corridor outside my room. The window looked out on the roof of the house across the street, where two workmen who were doing repairs ogled me shamelessly. It is true that I was somewhat underdressed. There could be no doubt that the enormous oil slick which was Mao's China—clean, polite, honest, prudish and conventional—had not spread as far as Canton!

After lunch Yuan took me aside and expressed regret for the morning's incident, stressing the fact that it was nothing to do with him and reminding me that nothing of the sort had happened in the North, under his jurisdiction. I jumped at the opportunity and told him emphatically that I was more than satisfied with his co-operation and his admirable efficiency, that I was very grateful to him for both help and efficiency, and that I had not failed to note the difference between North and South. Shu, standing with her hands in her pockets, broke in spitefully:

'We'll never be able to do anything with these southerners. They don't even speak a language we can understand.'

Subsequent events would prove Shu right. The Cultural Revolution was to have its work cut out in the South, and Shanghai would even become a rebel city.


A visit to an ivory workshop: a series of rooms on three floors in which sixty workers were cutting, etching and chiselling blocks of ivory with the same accuracy and precision as a Swiss watchmaker. In each room a 'creator' drew the model which the other workers then carved straight from the piece of ivory. These models were always traditional designs. Many of the workers were smoking, and their faces looked hollow and tired. A few of the women wore gold wedding rings. The men's vests often had holes in them. On the other hand, despite the heat, there were no bad smells anywhere in the workshop.

In the same street we watched children coming out of school: they formed an orderly swarm, without any running or shouting. Hosts of 'pioneers', or star pupils, wearing red neckerchiefs, stared at me inquisitively but without any sign of friendliness.

In the evening the farewell dinner took place. A speech by Yuan, a speech by the director of tourism in Canton, and two speeches by me. My appreciative group, after generously punctuating every tirade with *kampeis*, was roaring drunk, frantically applauded every sentimental passage, roared with laughter at my least printable jokes, and was shedding a few tears when the grilled pig was brought in, its head hanging to one side.

This was the great delicacy of Cantonese cuisine, cut into small pieces and put together again. Watched and encouraged by my Chinese friends, to whom I had just sworn eternal friendship, I caught a piece of the complicated jigsaw puzzle between my chopsticks. Under the skin, all I found was a small square piece of fat.

'At least they've removed the bristles!' Isabella whispered to me.

I shut my eyes and swallowed the lot. A gulp of warm wine, and on to the next course. Once the pig had been removed, I could open my eyes again and breathe in the warm breeze from the River of Pearls.

# 23

At dawn the next day, we were all ahead of time, in a hurry to leave the paradise that was Canton. We settled down on our last Chinese train, two by two and face to face. Three hours of paddy-fields and market-gardens, hills, half-naked peasants, and women in parasol-hats. I gazed hard at everything to commit it to memory. The loudspeaker on the train was emitting a shrill caterwauling. I protested.

'There are some people here who want to hear the radio,' replied Shin, who was usually friendlier than this.

There was a muddle over the exit formalities. Shin got into a panic, and he and the relevant official lost their way among all the orders and counter-orders. They ended up asking me for my visa to ... Hong Kong.

At the frontier we had a very good lunch in a pleasantly cool room. I changed my group's surplus currency and watched in fascination as the balls on the Chinese abacus performed frenzied dances. As I was rather worried about customs, I had taken the precaution of telling Yuan about my anxieties. A good many members of the party had suitcases crammed with antiques: did he think we would be kept a long time in customs? That would be terribly inconvenient, since we had to catch the train for Hong Kong which left the frontier post at one-fifteen. Yuan replied through Shin that I had no need to worry. He had warned the frontier post in advance.

'We shall get through without any trouble.'

Good. Still, one never knows. Georges's bag was bulging with old Chinese paintings. Madame Neralinda, the insatiable Peruvian, had had to buy three suitcases in Shanghai to carry her countless knick-knacks. Almost everybody in the party, except for Adrienne who 'hated that sort of thing', had bought dozens of Chinese antiques, all marked with the red wax seal which signified that an object could be exported. We walked in single file past two nonchalant, navy-blue customs men. All of us, except for ... Heavens! They had stopped Boilèle and led him into a little side-room. They let the others go through but beckoned to Madame Trollan, who joined Boilèle. I rushed after them. Boilèle, very genial with the Chinese, snarled at me *mezzo voce*:

'So this is how you look after our interests! You might at least have spared me this! Fortunately I am the Swedish Consul in Lyons and they can't get away with this.'

For the moment, however, they seemed to be 'getting away with this' quite successfully. Three more customs officials, one a middle-aged man who spoke good English, started removing all the knick-knacks from the General's suitcases, one by one, and then unwrapping them and lining them up side by side like a row of toy soldiers. Boilèle tried arguing, but for once without shouting. Madame Trollan did her best to calm him down. In the presence of the little customs men he was unusually quiet. The operation went on for a quarter of an hour, half an hour ... I turned anxiously to Yuan.

'I'm afraid we may miss our train,' I said.

Smiling as blandly as ever, but this time with a gleam in his eyes which was the nearest thing to malice that I had ever seen in him, Yuan reassured me:

'Don't worry, Madame Modiano, it will soon be over.'

It was one o'clock. At five past one the customs men shut the last of Boilèle's suitcases. The oldest official apologized to me for the delay and informed me that he was keeping three articles whose wax seals had apparently dropped off. He explained to Boilèle, who was fulminating that 'this was sheer robbery', that without their seals these articles could not leave China. This was a flagrant injustice, but I couldn't help finding it funny, since Boilèle and his Trollan had given me a hard time of it during the past month. The General snarled at the impassive Chinese that thanks to his diplomatic status he expected to receive the confiscated articles in Hong Kong in less than three days. In the corridor leading to the no man's land between the two frontiers, the farther he got from the customs house, the louder and more indignant his voice became. The silence of his companions was almost tangible. Only a minute earlier, they had all been rocking with laughter in this same corridor, and joking with our Chinese interpreters. Boilèle's tempers had not been entirely useless, I told myself, dragging my bag along behind my flock. They had succeeded in reconciling Chinese and Europeans and getting them to laugh together—and laughing together is a first step towards understanding one another.

At the end of the corridor there was a covered area about a hundred yards long: the no man's land between China and Hong Kong. The time had come to say goodbye. Each of us in turn shook hands with our guides, with more or less warmth depending on the person's character and the relations he or she had had with the Chinese. The Three Musketeers, Laure, Colette, the Chapeaus, the Blums and the Adjoufs had a friendly word of thanks for each one. Watching the scene, I reflected that these three human beings had just spent a whole month with us, with the sole object of pleasing us and satisfying the to them incomprehensible whims of a bunch of frequently selfish and discourteous capitalists. Yet they had become integrated to some extent with our party, not in any material sense, but emotionally. When Isabella took his hand in hers, Shin blushed and looked down. Afterwards he followed her with his eyes. Adrienne, Boilèle, Madame Trollan were cold and haughty and made a point of not thanking the Chinese, who bowed and smiled politely all the same.

When at last it came to my turn, Yuan squeezed my hands as if he would never stop and said something to me in Chinese. Shin, who had tears in his eyes, was so overwhelmed that he forgot to translate what Yuan had said, and told me:

'I hope that you will show me Paris one day.'

Shu, dear grumpy Shu, stood on tiptoe and did something unknown in China but which she had seen us do among ourselves: she kissed me on both cheeks. Her eyes were misty, and I too was beginning to feel a lump in my throat. I picked up my bag and walked away quickly. When I reached the end of the no man's land, I turned round for the last time and saw the three little figures in the distance waving tirelessly. The others had already disappeared. I stood still and gave a final wave. Then I went off to return to my facile, easy, life, deeply moved, and feeling as if I were deserting them. Which was illogical, for they were products of the Revolution which had given a direction to their lives. All three of them were satisfied with their lot and could not imagine any other, yet they went on waving to me, to me whom they were fond of, true, but possibly also to some vaguely glimpsed freedom, or perhaps simply to the idea of 'getting out', of 'seeing somewhere else' as Shin said to me one day.

On the other side, no more soft caps but khaki shorts, black socks, and English voices. In the train a steward came along with whisky and cigarettes. Within five minutes the atmosphere was that of a cocktail party. An unrecognizable, smiling Signora Negri went from one compartment to another, toasting the occupants. From the train I could see roads and cars, and the Chinese women in the stations had tight skirts, slit up to the thigh, high-heeled shoes, bouffant hair-styles, and a graceful, provocative walk. They were the sisters of the women we had just left, yet what a difference! The scenery too was similar, but nothing was the same. I felt rather sad.

At the Mandarin Hotel I found luxury, a marble bathroom, a cinemascopic view of one of the most beautiful bays in the world, letters posted in Paris two days before, a hairdresser, a pedicure, and a little perky-faced page-boy of seven who reminded me of other Chinese children but who, unlike them, expected a tip.

In the evening, in the bar, there were a few of us, not many, who sat silently over our glasses of whisky, feeling a little ashamed of all this luxury and noise, and thinking of our three friends who were waiting in the dingy Canton hotel for the morning train which in three days' travelling on hard seats would take them back to Peking, to go on with their life's work, the building of the People's China.

# INDEX